Fire and Faith:
Finding
Forgiveness

Wayne A. Kimball
Jr.
(AKA Joey)

Fire and Faith

Fire and Faith

Fire and Faith:

Finding Forgiveness

By Wayne A. Kimball Jr. (Joey)

First Edition Paperback

Cover and internal layout design by Fire 2 Faith Publishing LLC.

Publisher:

Fire 2 Faith Publishing, LLC

11971 N. 83rd Dr. Peoria, Arizona 85345

fire2faithpublishing@gmail.com

Book Design: Fire 2 Faith Publishing, LLC

Editors: Deborah Kimball

Cover Photos: Breanne Marie Kimball

http://breannekimball.wix.com/breesphotography

Library of Congress Control Number:

ISBN-10:0989561003
ISBN-13: 978-0989561006
Printed and bound in the United States of America

Fire and Faith

Dedication

This book is dedicated to my Father in Heaven!

Fire and Faith

Glory Be To God!

I want say thank you to my biological father, and step dad as well.

I say this because we, as children of God, are all here to serve Him.

If things in my life were different or better,

then it would have robbed God of His glory.

Fire and Faith

Special Thank you

First and, foremost: thanks to God for being with me on this journey through the past, present and future. I would like to thank my wife and children for staying with me through my struggles in life, and seeing me come out on the other side. Thank you Breanne for the cover photos to this book. Thank you, Morgan for the poem that you wrote. Thank you, Audra for the hand drawn picture of the family, and how you see us. I want thank my mother, who I know loves me very much and who I love as well. "Dream on" mom! Thank you to my grandfather, who never got to read this and my grandmother who has been a huge help in life. I would like to thank Paul and William for judging me in my worse times, and always accepting of me. I would also like to thank Owen and Barbara for never turning their backs on me. Thank you to the prettiest sister in law Becky. I would like to thank Men of Valor, "Paul Crouch," Don McCrea, Don McCrea Sr. for all the prayers as well as all the men that are my brothers in MOV. I would like to thank my good friend Winden Trimble for being just like a real brother would be, through disagreement and good times. Thank you to Frank Ward for the chase around the mailbox. Thank you to Tim Vendlinski for being a friend of mine and a great boss. Thank

Fire and Faith

you, Rob and Dee for being great friends to my family. A special thank you to the Governor of Arizona Jan Brewer and John Brewer for their kind words to me, and giving me direction. Thank you to Elizabeth Macdonald at Thunderbird Global School of Management for showing me the ropes of publishing. Thank you to Jose Alvarez for the ink work, and "skullies". I also would like to thank all the people that are in my life that helped make this possible; you all know who you are. I would also like thank Liberty University for my journey through school. Each professor helped me obtain the knowledge making it possible to write this book. If I have forgotten anyone, I apologize.

Fire and Faith

[28] "Come to Me, all who are weary and heavy-laden, and I will give you rest. [29] Take My yoke upon you and learn from Me, for I am gentle and humble in heart, and you will find rest for your souls. [30] For My yoke is easy and My burden is light."

Matthew 11:28-30

Fire and Faith

Preface

This recount of my past, and is not about my mother or father. In fact I hold my mother to the highest level of honor and I love her with all my heart. This is about what I remember and the mistakes I made in life. This book is about the damage I did to others, and myself. I also would like to share that there were good moments in my past as well, but I am going over the bad times. I would also like to share that it was the bad moments in my life that defined who I was until I learned about forgiveness.

It is about what I perceived, and what I went through. During the course of writing this book, I have done a lot of careful studying in the area of psychology and drug abuse. I have been able to uncover a lot of truth about myself and learn how to manage the different problems that I had developed over the course of my life. Not only have I been able to [now] manage these problems, but I have also been able to heal from many of them as well. There is great deal of information that is not in this book that has to do with members of my family, but because of my education, I realized that the information that was left out had no real importance to what I became. Some would argue this point, but I am comfortable with what I have said. This is also not an excuse as to why I grew up and did the bad things that I did. Some people say that "you

Fire and Faith

are lucky to be alive." When I hear the horror stories of other people though, they seem to have it a lot worse than me. Nevertheless, I believe my story is worth sharing. You see, I have been physically abused, mentally abused, abandoned, addicted to drugs, raped by two different men, and homeless. All of this took place before the age of 15. I believe it is vitally important to have to go back to the beginning in order to understand the end. I will also continue to explain the path of self-destruction I was on as I grew older, and how I was able to find forgiveness for myself and others.

Chapter 1

I was born in 1969 during the Vietnam War. I was an only child, and the only grandson on my mother's side. My father was away fighting in the war during the time I was born. During his time there in Vietnam he would send home stereo equipment (i.e. speakers). He would also send instructions telling my mother not to open the boxes, and that he would open them when he came home. Come to find out, he had shipped marijuana home inside the speakers. When my father returned to the states he came home to his wife, speakers filled with pot, and a newborn son. I cannot even imagine what that man had to go through while he was in Vietnam. What I do know is that it was horrific. So when you combine his upbringing and the war you end up with a person with many struggles. I just want to let everyone know that the choices I made are not excuses because of what my father did to me, by any means.

I was a baby, and like most babies I cried, giggled, was hungry, messed my diaper, and was inquisitive about the world. The problem was that my father was not ready to deal with this, and if you ask my mother, she would tell you that my father was not convinced that I was his son. I believe truly that this was part of the reason why my father treated me as he did. I also know that my father was abused as a child as well. His father was a horrible man to my dad. I remember one of the stories my father told me when I was very young was when my father was young, he had a cat that he loved dearly. One day, when school the day came to an end, he rushed home as fast as he could to his cat. When my father could not find the cat, he asked his father where it was. His father's response was that it was in the back yard. So my father ran out the back door to find that his dad had hung the cat from a wire.

This will tell you a little something about the hell my father went through, and may explain a little about how (and why) he treated me as he did. The problem was he was hurt as a child and he was so wounded he never forgave. I believe with all my heart that if he had found forgiveness, he himself would be in a better place. Even to this day he still refuses to acknowledge that I am his son, and refuses to talk to me. However I have forgiven him and I put my faith in God that He has a plan for that part of my life.

When I would cry, (as babies do), he would tell my mother to "Leave him alone. He has to get tough." He would also say, "If you run to him every time he cries, then he will never stop crying for attention". On one particular occasion, it was late at night and I'd been crying pretty hard for some time, all the while, my father telling my mother not to check on me. He told her that I would eventually stop, but I didn't. It had been raining long and hard that night, and the roof had been leaking. After listening to me cry in my room for such a long time, my mother decided, to hell with my father and said, "I am going to checking on him." What she found was that the roof had leaked and had come through the ceiling of my room. Part of the ceiling had caved in on my baby crib. I was not hurt, but you can imagine a baby's fear. When my mother got to me I was soaking wet from the rain and (I am) sure I was a little cold.

By the age of two, my life with him did not getting any better; in fact things were getting even worse. We lived in a mobile home. The only thing my father was interested in was his fast cars, and tormenting me. At some point, (according to my father), I fell off the roof and broke my leg. I have to say though, I don't know too many 2 year olds that get up onto a roof, let alone fall off. The truth is I believe my father had me up there with him, and he was not paying attention and I fell off. If you ask members of my family, they would say I was pushed. If the only incident had been a broken leg, I probably would have been fine, but it wasn't.

Fire and Faith

In my mother and fathers room there used to be a fuse panel that looked a lot like a face. In my eyes, I imagined this face was some kind of "boogie man", and my father was all about playing this up to me. He and his friends would get together, and after a few beers, he thought it was fun to scare the hell out of me. He would plug a microphone into his stereo, and make me walk down the hallway to go see "the box." (The boogie man had a name, and it was "the box." This was totally against my will and I was scared to death. The walk (to me at the time) from the living room down the hallway seemed like it took forever to get there. As I would start my way down the long dark hallway towards their bedroom, I could see a slight glow coming from their lamp on the nightstand. At times I would be so scared that I would pee my pajamas. I knew if I ran back scared to the living room with pee in my pajamas, there would be hell to pay. As I walked down the hallway, my father would be saying in a deep voice, "Closer, closer, closer, WATCH OUT! It's THE BOX!" As I ran down the hallway back to my room I would hear my father and his friends laughing. This type of torment and scaring started severe night terrors that continued into my adult life.

The beatings I suffered as a baby were bad enough that every part of my body from the neck down was black and blue. I obviously do not

Fire and Faith

remember this, but my grandmother told me stories of my past. On one occasion at a family get together, I messed my diaper, and the women in my small family rallied together to change it. I know it sounds strange, but I was the first born child to the family, and the only grandson. When they began removing my clothing was when the physical damage was revealed. My grandmother, aunt, great aunt and mother were all in the room at the time. I am sure my mother was very uncomfortable. On one hand she was trying to protect me, but on the other trying to protect the man she loved.

My family would get together at my grandmother's house for barbeques a lot during the summer. This was a time for me to get away from my father and seek protection from the rest of the family. I knew that when people came to visit or we went to visit other people, he could not be the tyrant that he was at home. In fact there was a time that I actually hid the coats of the visitors so they could not leave. I took the coats and wedged them on the back side of the bed against the wall, and would play dumb as to their location. In my mind if they could not find their coats, they could not leave. I can remember a couple of times where my father slipped and showed his ugly (mean) side. On this occasion the whole family was in the pool at my grandparents' house. It was summer day, and I did not want anything to do with the big pool. My grandparents bought a little" kiddie" pool, that was about a foot deep. It was plenty deep for me considering I could not swim. Somehow or other I got too close to the big pool and fell in. I remember slowly sinking to the bottom as I struggled to get to the surface. I could see the legs of my father just out of reach. He was facing me and I really expected him to save me, but he did not. I slowly sank to the bottom of the pool, I remember seeing a rush of bubbles all around me, and two arms outstretched reaching for me. I was grabbed forcefully and brought to the top of the water. I remember crying, because of the unfamiliar feeling of the water that went up my nose and down my throat, not to mention the sheer terror of drowning. I remember the water burned as it entered my nose and throat; much like when you laugh too hard while drinking a soda. I remember my grandmother yelling at my father, calling him every name in the book, because he did nothing to help me.

My mother's family was Irish Catholic. My father, on the other hand, grew up as an atheist. As a small boy however, I did not understand the meaning of atheist. What I did know was that I would go to Sunday school and sing about God and learn about Jesus, and were also taught about the devil as well. Many of us know about the Catholic religion and its' rules and regulations (at least it was when I

Fire and Faith

was growing up). My father love to play mental games with me. At times in fact, I think he thrived on it. At night (when he was around) he would tell me about the devil, and how he would come and get me at night while I slept. At the same time, I would remember what I was taught at church and from my mother about God. What a confusing time this was for me. I did not know who to pray to. I remember my mother and I would pray to God, telling him that I love him just before bedtime. Just after my mother left my room and shut out the light, I would pray to the devil as well and tell him that, I loved him too. It is very clear to me that I did not want to upset either one.

Just before falling asleep, I would shut my closet doors, because I was told by my father that if the devil was mad at me that he would come through the doors at night while I slept. Sometimes in the middle of the night, I would wake up to see the closet doors slightly open. At the time, I believed that my prayer to the devil was not sufficient, and that he was upset with me. I was truly in fear and that was the way my father liked it. I believed that the devil was in my room watching me sleep.

I did not know what the devil would do to me, but according to my father it was not going to be good. Now, it is a safe assumption that the devil really did not open the door. That left my father as the one who

Fire and Faith

opened it. Nevertheless, I felt as if that the devil was really mad at me no matter what I did. When someone is bad to a child, they possess a higher power than a good person. I say this because a good person was never able to rescue me. It seemed to me that the "bad" ruled my life.

We lived in a home on the East Coast, in the town of Hudson, Massachusetts. I was not allowed in the house during the day if my father was home. On some occasions when my mother was home, or if we had company, then I was allowed in. My father always tried to play the "model parent" in front of everybody. Everyone knew he was full of crap, but they did nothing about it. In fact most bad things that happened in my childhood could have been prevented, but weren't. I also believe the most confusing thing for me was seeing him act like the model parent in front of company.

I always wondered why he could not be like that all the time. The truth is, when my father was home and, there was no company, I was not allowed to be in the same room as he was. To a little boy, that was one of the most devastating feelings thinking that my own father did not want me around. All my other friends had a better relationship with the parents and I could not figure out why my relationship was so different. In my house I just knew that the living room was very dark, and 70'Ss rock and roll music played at a loud volume.

Fire and Faith

On rare occasions I can remember being allowed in the living room while the Boston Bruins hockey game was on. My parents were big time hockey fans and so was I. When the game was on, I could get away with coming out to see the game. To be perfectly honest those nights seem to be the happiest for me. I remember trying to sit close to my father with my arm just close enough to touch the hairs on his arm. I just wanted to be close to him and every time he would either move away or, tell me to get the hell away from him.

When I think about it now, I really did not like the hockey games, and I surely was not a fan. Even through all the crap, I was just a child that craved his father affection. I believe I was just looking for a place to fit in. Most of the homes had a cellar. Of course, I was told that the devil (and any other type of evil) would lurk in a darkened cellar and wait there for me. This particular house had a side door that led into the cellar and, of course, the only way to enter. My bike and Big-Wheel had to be parked in the cellar. In the morning it was easy to get my toys out because a little ray of sunshine slipped in through the tiny window, and the gaps around the sides of the door. But at the end of the day, and it became dark, it was a completely different story.

Fire and Faith

The only real social activity I had was when I was with my friends during the day. I always seemed to be alone when the sun went down. The rest of the attention came from my mother when my father was not around. Though, for the most part, I was in my room alone with a haunting feeling at all times. I spent a lot of time in my bedroom and, to be truthful, there was not a lot to do. I knew that I hated it though. My imagination would run wild with "boogie man" thoughts.

When I was about 4 years old, my attention span was short, so I often found myself bored. My imagination would run crazy, and I would envision horrible, evil, dark, creatures hiding in the shadows of my room. Right next to the door of my bedroom was a tall, free-standing, black lamp. I would drag the step-stool in my room to the tall lamp and get as close to the light as I could. I truly feared the dark areas of my room. One of the things I would do to keep myself from focusing on this evil, was to lick paper and place it on the hot light bulb. You see, if the paper became moist and was placed on the hot light bulb, it would steam. There was a certain odor that came along with it. Now that I think of it, it was quite disgusting. If I kept myself busy, I would not focus on my fears as much. Never the less, it was something to do. To this day, I have a problem holding newsprint paper because of the texture, and the haunting thought of the smell.

Fire and Faith

There were times when my mother was not home, and I was left with my father. Those times were very rare. During these times he would not let me into the house, and I was not allowed to have any food or drink. I know what everyone is thinking while reading this, "why didn't he just drink from the hose outside. Believe me, I thought of that. But, he would watch to make sure I didn't. I never saw him in the windows watching but, he always knew. On one particular night after having a day like I just described, my mother came home, and made dinner.

Now, I was about five years old. And, like any other five year old, I was picky. Actually, I don't even know if it was an issue of being picky. I think it was more an issue of being so hungry that everything sounded bad to me. I know now that when I go without food for a long period of time, like most people, I become indecisive about what sounds good to eat. On this particular evening my appetite was just that. I did not want what my mother was serving and I refused to eat it. At his point my mother offered to make something else for me but, my father decided to send me off to bed instead. He was pissed-off thinking that my mother was going to do something nice for me and, he decided that no food was the better option.

Fire and Faith

I went off to bed crying and hungry, still not knowing what I wanted to eat. But, it didn't matter because I was not allowed to eat. I tried to sleep but, my hunger grew. I could smell the brownies my mother was baking in the oven. (And to be truthful, *that* is what I wanted to eat.) But, I knew that if I got up, I would take a whipping from my dad, so I stayed in bed. I'd had enough whippings from his leather belt and, I did not want the bruising or bleeding (on occasion) on my back-side. It was not enough for him to hit me once or twice. It was always seven or more hits. I can still see him now standing tall over me and, telling me to turn around. If I got into any kind of trouble, I would always have to take the punishment in my room. On the way to my room from the living room, was a long hallway. I can remember doing anything I could to not to go down the hallway. One time, I went so far as to tie my shoe just to try and prolong the inevitable.

Eventually, after laying there for what seemed like hours to me, I finally fell asleep. It was not long before I woke to a silent house. The silence meant that my mother and father had fallen asleep, and this was my opportunity to get something to eat. My mother had left the freshly baked brownies on top of the oven, and this was my chance to get some. I was not tall enough to see the top of the stove, but if I reached far enough, I could get the tips of my fingers across the top of the brownies. Unfortunately, at the age of five, I did not consider the thought of being caught. I was able to drag my fingers across the top of the brownies and eat what stuck on my fingertips. I ate just enough to satisfy my hunger.

I woke that morning to my father grabbing me by the back of my hair and dragging me down the hallway as if I were a dog that just messed on the floor. I was put down in a chair and the pan of brownies was placed in front of me. I was repeatedly asked over and over again if I had eaten them. I was scared to death to answer the question considering how he was treating me. I knew that I would be punished severely if I admitted it. The evidence was obvious. My fingers matched the lines across the top of brownies. I remember my mother pleading with my father saying that "it is no big deal, I can make more." He yelled at me and said "You want them? Then you eat them!" My mother was very upset that he was making me eat them. But, my father would have no part of that, and he forced me to eat the whole pan. On any other day that would have sounded like a lot of fun, but this day was straight torture. After eating the fourth one, I started to feel sick. It was not long before I vomited, but he continued to make me eat them. I was told if I did not eat them, he was going to force them down my throat. My poor mother had to clean up the mess as I

Fire and Faith

continued to eat and throw up. I knew my mother was not happy but, I genuinely felt she figured she was trapped.

The abuse was not just directed toward me. I later found out that my father would come home and perform a "white glove" inspection on the house. He would literally walk through our house with his fingers touching all the hidden areas looking for dirt. When she did not pass the inspection, she was threatened to be sold to white slavery. As I mentioned before, I was not allowed into the same room with them. The stereo was always loud enough that, I could not hear what was going on, or what was being said between the two of them. I can only imagine the insults and threats he made to my mother. Every once in a while I would hear her crying.

In the beginning, I always believed that the both of them must have hated me. It was complete confusion for me and, I always carried the belief that everything was my fault. I remember one afternoon my father was in the bathroom and I really needed to use the bathroom. I remember knocking at the door, and my father yelling at me to go away. I was only four at the time and when a four year old has to go to the bathroom, it generally means they have to go right then. I remember going back into my bedroom but, I could not wait anymore. I went back to the bathroom door and told my father that I had to go poop, and that I needed to go right then. I remember him yelling at me to go away and that I better not mess my pants. I could not stand it and before I knew it, I'd messed my pants. I started crying as I was messing my pants, and he heard me. He knew what I had done, and when he got out of the bathroom he shoved me into the bathroom to clean myself up. After I got out, he was waiting there for me with the belt. My mother was so pissed at him but, it was not enough to stop him from giving me the belt.

He treated her in a bullying manner as well. That was the first time I witnessed it. Eventually it became clear to me that if he could be that mean to me, then he must be that mean to her. As I grew older, the thought steadily crept into my head that she could not protect me. At one point, I actually thought of walking in his room while he slept, and hitting him with my mother's cast iron pan. However, I knew that would not be a good idea. I felt all alone and abandoned. I could never be good enough or loving enough to change my father's thoughts toward me. For a five year old, that was a lot of burden to take on. This type of belief haunted me in every avenue of my life until my late 30's.

Chapter 2

It was not until I was about 7 years old that my mother and father were well on their way to getting divorced. I hate to say it, but it was a wonderful day for me. I knew that if my father was not in the picture, I would not have to endure his constant infliction of pain. The last night he and I were together we were alone. Normally, for me, this would not turn out well. I was in constant fear that sooner or later I would take a whipping or endure some kind of abuse. This time, it was strange though. We had a cheeseburger, french-fries, and a cold beer for dinner. He was absolutely nice to me. Every bit of kindness that I'd ever wanted from my father was revealed to me that night. I know the beer was not right for a 7 year old. But his conversation with me was one that I believed a father and son would share. He was nice to me and, for a brief moment, I thought I actually had a dad. Soon after that I went to bed and, had the best night sleep that any child could ever have.

The court hearing was approaching, and my mother and I were leaving to go stay with my grandparents. During the court hearing the judge asked about the property and all the personal items in the house. They were able to work out how things were to be divided. The judge

Fire and Faith

then asked about their child. The first response was from my mother who said, "I want my son." My father responded that 'he wanted the dog, and he did not want me because, I was not his son'. At the end of the proceeding, everything was supposed to be divided equally between my parents. My mother and I left shortly after that to visit my grandparents in Arizona. We stayed with them for a couple of weeks and when we returned home, found that my father had taken everything from the house. I remember looking up at my mother and she was heartbroken. He had taken everything, even the toilet paper in the bathroom. I think the most warped thing through all of this was that I knew what kind of man my father was yet I still wanted his love and affection. I would actually defend his name when my mother or grandparents would talk badly about him.

After dealing with not having a dime to her name and, nowhere to go, my mother somehow got a few dollars together to get us an apartment. We were not there long, and before we knew it, we were moving again, and again. At one point we moved to Marlboro, Massachusetts. This (to me) was a great place to live. We lived right across the hall of my aunt and uncle. To me, my uncle was what I wanted in a dad and, to this day I still go over to his house and feel like his son. I remember I would stay with them quite often. We used to

Fire and Faith

watch wrestling, (back when Hulk Hogan was starting his career). The

Hulk was the biggest name in wrestling. My uncle and I also had

another favorite show: The Incredible Hulk. I am not sure if my uncle

really liked it, but he made me feel like he did. That is something I will

always love him for. We moved one more time before ending up in an

apartment in a really bad part of town in Lowell, Massachusetts.

However, when you are a kid it really does not seem that bad.

My mother got a job working as a parts driver and made fifty dollars

a week. We lived on spaghetti noodles and, on good nights we added

ketchup for sauce. I was proud of my mother for doing everything she

could to take care of us. To this day I don't think she knows how much

I love her for that. We had each other, and for me that was enough. I

knew my mother and I were struggling to make ends meet. But, at the

same time it seemed to be the "norm" to some degree.

My mother would go to work every morning and bust her butt, to

make sure that there was food in the cupboard. I remember one time I

took fifty dollars out of her wallet to "strike it rich". At that time,

lottery scratcher tickets had just come out. I thought if I bought the

right ticket, we would be rich and I would be able take my mother away

from all the crap and garbage living where we did. Unfortunately, I

was unsuccessful with the scratchers. The worst part was explaining to my mother about the fifty dollars. To make it even worse she was planning on taking me to the circus as a surprise. See, little did I know, that was her bonus from work.

Our apartment was below the first floor. When you looked out our window you would see the feet of people walking by. If you have ever seen the sitcom "Laverne and Shirley", our apartment was a lot like that. Across the street from the apartment was a bread factory. I can still smell the fresh-baked bread now. On Saturday mornings I would get up at about four o'clock and go to help unload the bread trucks. At eight years old, they obviously could not pay me money, so they paid me in loaves of bread and snack cakes. What a great job! Some would call that "child slavery" but, I called it payday!

Eventually I started getting to know the other kids at the apartment where we lived. They were a few years older than I was. We started getting into trouble as most boys do. I started sneaking out at night to hang out at the bar with my friends that lived just down the road. In fact one night after work my mother went for a drink with co-workers after work, and the bartender asked my mother "Do you have a son?" She replied, "Yes I do." The bartender said "He comes in here about ten o'clock at night." She was in total disbelief. Later that night, I snuck out and met up with the boys, and headed to the bar. I was not

Fire and Faith

Where we lived, there was a set of train tracks that ran alongside the Merrimack River, just behind our apartment complex. Joe and I would take coins and place them on the railroad tracks, and wait for the train. The train would pass by and flatten the coins. The biggest challenge was to find the coins after they had been run over. Eventually, we started thinking about how fun it would be to hop on the trains and ride to other towns. Eventually this thought became the new challenge: to run fast enough to be able to grab the bars on the side of the train car, and pull ourselves on.

We used to grab for the box cars, because they were much easier to grab on to. Once we were on the train we would climb up the side ladders and get to the top of the box cars, then sit on top and pretend we were the engineers. While the train was moving at its fastest, we stand up and feel the wind in our faces. What a rush! We actually rode a train from Lowell, Massachusetts all the way to the state of New Hampshire. My mother was so upset when she got the call from the state police. She had to drive all the way there to pick me up. This game came to end one day when we entered a box car and there were hobos inside. They were not friendly at all and we had to jump from the box car while it was on the move. Believe it or not, we were quite

Fire and Faith

scared. That railroad track was my way of being free from all the hurt and pain.

We soon discovered that riding our bikes was a much safer way to play and, it seemed like much less trouble. We would ride all over town and, thought we owned the world. Everything (in our minds) was meant for us to either wreck or take. One day, Joe and I were coming back to our apartments on our bikes because it was starting to get late. The sun was just starting to go down. To get home faster we used to cut through the front yard of an old man that lived near the apartments. On this day though, I had no idea what was about to happen. Joe was ahead of me on his bike and, I could see ahead of him that there was a white car parked with the passenger door open. At the same time I spotted a girl my age picking wild flowers in the yard that we used to cut through. Joe was not slowing down. The girl was bent down with a pretty dress on and a handful of flowers in her hand. She was absolutely beautiful to me. Joe kept up at full speed and ran over part of her dress, knocking the flowers out of her hand. I had to stop. I just could not go by and be the cold hearted, destructive little boy that I was used to being. I stopped to help her pick up the flowers. I could only stare at her and, say sorry over and over again. She was the prettiest girl I had ever seen and, she was not from our part of town.

Fire and Faith

She was from the upscale side of Lowell. Lowell was divided into two parts. She was from the pretty area of town with all the nice homes and cars. My side of town had the not so pretty houses and not so pretty cars. I did not care though; to me the town was mine. She asked me my name, and I told her "Joey." Sadly, I still cannot remember her name. I did not want to stop looking at her, but her mother was calling her back to the car for them to leave. To me she made my not so pretty part of town beautiful. As I got back on my bike, and watched her mother drive her away, I thought to myself that this was the best day of my life. To this day, I still think of that little girl and, hope that she is doing well in life. How would I know that this day was going to be one of the worst?

When I returned home my mother was standing outside of the apartment with her hands on her hips and, her head at a slight tilt. I thought to myself I must be in trouble for being late or, for something else. As I got closer to her, I could see a smile on her face. She looked different and, happier than I'd seen her in a long time. My mother brought me into the apartment and told me to get cleaned up because we were going to her friend's apartment for dinner. I did not understand why I needed to get cleaned up to go over there. I mean, come on, we had been there many times. It was my friend Joe's

apartment. It was right across the hall. What was the big deal?

When we got to the apartment, there was a man there that I did not

recognize. My mother immediately sat next to him as if they were

longtime friends. My mother asked me to come closer, and she

introduced me to him. Apparently they had been seeing each other for

a couple of days. Little did I know that he was going to be with us for a

very long time. I ended up staying the night at that apartment. I could

hear the adults out in the living room having a good time. Everyone

was laughing, the music was somewhat loud and, the smell of cigarettes

was the only smell in Joe's room. Joe was talking to me about how

cool it would be if my mom and Bob got married. If they did get

married that would make Joe and I cousins. That is when I realized,

that Bob was my mom's friends brother.

In a way I thought it would be neat to have a cousin with the same

name as me that lived right across the hall. I still had no idea where

this man was from though. I just assumed he would be staying with us.

In some weird kind of way however, it was a little unsettling for me. It

had been my mom and I for the past couple of years and, I did not want

a man wrecking it for us. I had trust issues with men; mainly because

of my father but, also due to the recent rape by the babysitter. Just as I

Chapter 4

The trip was miserable, hot, and long. We drove for hours and hours which seemed like days to me. I was only eight, and everything to an eight year old is long and miserable if they don't like what they are doing. I finally fell asleep during the last part of the trip. I remember my mother waking me up to say that we made it. The first thing I did was grab my six-gun and strap on my holsters and cowboy hat. I had it all planned out in my head. I was going out into his farm and getting on a horse. In my mind I was going to meet kids similar to the ones that I met in Arizona. I also had thoughts that I was going to have a childhood similar to what I just discovered in Arizona with my grandparents, but that was not the case. When I cleared the sleep from my eyes I realized that there was no farm. There were no horses, chickens, goats or, cattle. The only thing alive that I saw was a single cow in a neighbor's yard about a half-mile away. Bobs house was a single-wide, broken-down, old trailer sitting alongside of a hill. My immediate thought was that this man was a liar, and he was no different from my father.

We started to unpack what little bit my mother and I had. I brought everything I owned into my 5'x7' room. I remember we did not have any furniture at all in the house accept 2 beds. There was no living room furniture, so we used pillows to sit on. My mom was in the kitchen making dinner and once again it was not something I wanted to eat. My mother has always had this desire to please the man she is with; even it means sacrificing herself in the process. I remember we sat at the dinner table and I ate everything but my beans. For some reason they tasted very different to me and I was not interested in eating them. Bob was insistent that I eat everything on my plate. I refused to eat them though. He told me I was not allowed to leave the table until I ate everything. Just like old times my mother did nothing. I sat there for an hour and a half determined not to eat them. I could hear my mother talking to Bob saying "Just let it go, let him leave the table." Eventually after he went off to the bathroom my mother quickly grabbed my plate and told me to go off to bed. I later heard him ask her "Did he finish his plate?" and she said "Yes." He came down the hallway, and looked in my room and asked "Was that so hard?" I did not respond I just laid there pretending that I was asleep.

There was not much to do in Lake Elsinore, California. And there were not a many kids near my house. I did meet a boy that lived across the field up on top of a hill. He was pretty cool and he was a year older than me. To me most of the kids there seemed backwards. They

Fire and Faith

almost seemed kind of dumb to me. However he did have a sister

named Maria that I thought was really neat. She was my age, in the

same grade, but she was also handicapped. Maria was born with a

disease where her bones did not grow. Therefore, she had difficulty

with the other kids picking on her. Being a midget was only a small

part of her condition. Maria's disease required multiple surgeries and

her body was covered with scars, but I thought she was the coolest

thing since sliced bread. Her personality was so bright that you just

had to love her. This disease would eventually take her life, and she

knew it. But, she was so positive that it made me think that my

problems were nothing compared to hers.

I spent most of my time over at their house because I knew that Bob

was not interested in me and, I was not interested in him. One of the

problems was I was not an athlete or into sports. But I also knew that

he was jealous for my mother's attention, and I only made things more

difficult. He made that very obvious when my mother was not

listening, or paying attention to him. He was the same as my father but,

this time I was sent outside and not to my room, at least in the

beginning. When I was home though, everything was about him. All

television was about him. It was always the news or some kind of

stupid sports program. In fact, because of this, I can't stand watching

Fire and Faith

sports to this day. That's probably a good thing though. He had my mother wait on him hand and foot. The only thing that he could accomplish on his own was going to the bathroom.

The rest of the summer finally passed, and it was time for school. The parents of my friends on the hill asked me if I would watch out for Maria because everyone made fun of her. When she walked it was more like a watching a penguin walk. She swayed side to side like a small, obese person. I am not making fun of her. I am trying to paint a picture of how she moved. Maria also wore shorts that showed the massive scars on her legs. The day I met her she had been crying because some of the neighbor kids had picked on her for being different. I realized quickly that she could not depend on her brother for help. I agreed with Maria's parents, and promised to look out for her. Not only was I going to a new school for the first time but, I was by Maria's side.

We all met first thing in the morning to catch the bus to school. The poking and joking started right off the bat, and it was not long before I had to punch some kid in the face. The word got around school quick and the joking and poking towards Maria stopped. I quickly made a name for myself and everyone knew that it was not cool to pick on Maria. I remember one time they had an open house at the school. The perfectly honest, I felt as if I had no value. That was not the first time, and it certainly would not be the last time.

My mother enrolled me into elementary school in Arizona. It was not too bad going to this school considering I already knew the neighborhood kids. My first day was going to be the following Monday. The school wasn't too far from my grandparent's house so I was able to walk there and back home. I was in the middle of 3rd grade. (This would be the 7th school I attended so, changing schools was very familiar to me.) I was at school one day and I was not feeling well so I went to the nurse's office. I had been feeling sick to my stomach, and the nurse decided that it would be best for me to go home. Nobody from the house could come to get me so I walked home. I was walking home when I noticed two men following me. I was scared right off the bat and, when they slowed to a near crawl, I started to get very nervous. I started to move a little quicker and I heard the van trying to catch up. One of the men kept telling me to come over to the van. By this point I was terrified! I ran as fast as I could to a house that was not mine. I acted like it was my house and walked straight in like I lived there. I only walked in about three steps, but it was good enough for the van to speed away.

Fire and Faith

Fortunately for me, the people that lived in the home were in the back yard. I truly believe now when I think about it, someone above was watching out for me. I could see the people through the living room window in the backyard doing work. I quietly opened the front door and stepped out and made my way home. My heart was racing, and I was out of breath by the time I got home. My mother was worried about how I was acting and, asked what happened. I told her the whole story and she told me that everything was going to be ok. I continued to walk to and from school, but with a group of kids. Safety in numbers is how my folks looked at it.

It was not long before I heard the words that we would be moving again. This time we were moving back east again. We were moving to Merrimack, New Hampshire. Only this time there would be something very different about the new house we were going to. Bob had an 18 year old daughter named Jackie. Jackie lived with Bob's ex-wife and she was too much for his ex-wife to handle. Jackie flew in to Phoenix, Arizona and, we picked her up to take her with us to Merrimack. I will never forget the first time I saw her. Being a boy at my age and due to my sexual dysfunctions, all I could do is stare at her large chest. I remember that she had the biggest well you know what I saying. She had a fowl mouth and, she smoked cigarettes constantly. It seemed like knocked again only louder and harder, and yet no reply. I told Gregory that he must not be home and that we should come back later. Gregory said, "Hang on." as he banged on the door harder. At that moment a man yelled from inside saying "Who is there? What do you want?!" I could hear the man's heavy footsteps as he came closer to the door.

He opened the door fast and hard as looked out side to side to see who was there. He was a large, fat man, and I immediately got the chills as I flashed back to my old baby sitter. He had a zippo lighter in his left hand, and he kept opening and closing the lid as he stared at Gregory and me. I could smell something in the apartment that smelled like trash, which had not been taken out in a few weeks. Finally, after what seemed like ten minutes he said to come in. As we walked in, I looked around and there was clutter everywhere. Every part of the room had some type of decoration or some type of object piled up. The place was cluttered beyond belief. Every part of the place had some type of object or clutter.

As I looked around I had seen that he had a porno on the television but the volume turned all the way down. To the left of me was the dining room with a bunch of newspapers, and penthouse magazines on the table. He told us to come into the dining room and sit down. As I walked into the dining room I looked to the right of me to the kitchen.

Fire and Faith

The sink was filled with dirty dishes, and the garbage I had smelled from the door was over flowing in the garbage can just left of the stove. The chairs at the table were straight-back vinyl with tears all along the back side of them, and on the seat cushions. They had been torn for quite a while because the vinyl was rolled and hard. I was wearing a pair of shorts and a tank top, and I remember it felt like it was digging into my shoulder and thighs. My back was to the kitchen and Gregory sat next to me. The fat man sat across the table facing Gregory and me. He sat there quiet and repeatedly opened and shut the Zippo lighter over and over again. He kept staring at me strange and finally he asked me if he knew me. I told him that we had never met.

Gregory finally spoke up and asked him if we could by a small bag of weed. He told us he only had little, but he would smoke some with us. The fat man told Gregory that he was getting more weed later that evening, and if he wanted some that he would take the money now, and he could pick it up later. Gregory reached in his pockets and realized that he had forgotten his money. Gregory said that he would run home and get it, and bring it right back. The fat man pulled a bag and pipe out of his pocket. He then filled the pipe with weed lit it with the zippo lighter. He passed the pipe to Gregory and then to me. I was so sketchy about being there that I decided to take big hit off the pipe to calm me down. We smoked that pipe about six times and I really felt stoned. In fact, I don't think I had ever been that high.

Everything seemed to be in slow motion and I felt somewhat tingly and numb at the same time. After being there for about twenty minutes, Gregory stood up and said that he would be right back. I started to get up as well to go with him and Gregory said "Stay here." He told me that if I went back with him that I would blow it, and his parents would know that I was high. I was not sure about staying, but the higher I felt, the more I figured it would be ok.

Gregory walked to the front door and opened it up, and the sunshine came through. The sun was so bright that it made my eyes squint even smaller than they already were. The door shut behind Gregory, and that was the last time I ever saw Gregory. The fat man asked if I wanted another hit off the pipe. I figured I was already high, why not get higher? The fat man got up out of his chair and sat down next to me where Gregory was sitting. He stood about six feet, two inches. He weighed about three hundred-twenty pounds. At the time, I was eleven and an average height for an eleven year old. I was built like a string bean. I started to feel real uncomfortable about how close he was sitting to me. At that moment, as I started to move my chair over and away, he wrapped both of his fat hands around my throat and neck. I started to pull away, but I could not get free. I continued to struggle, and that is when he said that he would kill me if I struggled anymore. He stood up with my neck in his hands, and dragged me down the hallway.

I remember being dragged, as the heels of my tennis shoes caught on the carpet and bounced up and down. I had one hand on his hand trying to pry his hands off, but he was squeezing so tight I could barely breathe. My other hand was dragging down the hallway wall. I could feel the paint from the wall building up underneath my fingernails. He brought me into the bedroom where he literally picked me up and threw me onto his bed. I tried to go off the other side of the bed to get out, but I was just not strong enough to get past him. He reached out again and caught me by the throat, and forced me backwards until my legs came out from underneath me. I fell back onto his bed, and before I could get any words out he punched me in the side of the head. He kept his hand on my throat while his other hand undid his own pants. I tried to get up again when he pushed my head into the head board of the bed. Once he got his pants down he reached for my shorts and was able to unbutton them and pulled them off. He kept saying that if I would be still he would not have to hurt me.

Fire and Faith

He laid his fat body on top of me, and I could barely breathe as the panic set in. He said that this would be over soon. He kept his hands around my throat as he performed oral sex on me. I told him I thought Gregory had returned, and was at the door. He said if it was him that he would come back later. I was looking for anything to make him stop, but it just wasn't working. Then he slid his fat sweaty body up on me and forced himself into me and stayed there until he finished. My panic soon turned into trying to side with him, and show him that I was not a threat. I told him over and over again that I needed to call home because I had to check in. He continued trying to finish what he was doing to me, and finally he did.

He asked me if I would like a towel to wipe the mess off of me. I told him that I needed to call home because that was most important. The strange thing was he allowed to me to make the call. I remember trying to dial the phone. It was the old style phone that was a rotary. My hands were shaking so hard I could not get my finger in the holes to dial. I finally was able to dial the phone and my mother answered the phone. I asked her what time dinner was, and when I needed to be home. The rule was that I was supposed to be home every night at 5:00. I just figured she would sense something was wrong by me calling. I never called to find out what time I needed to be home, so

Fire and Faith

Fortunately for me, the people that lived in the home were in the back yard. I truly believe now when I think about it, someone above was watching out for me. I could see the people through the living room window in the backyard doing work. I quietly opened the front door and stepped out and made my way home. My heart was racing, and I was out of breath by the time I got home. My mother was worried about how I was acting and, asked what happened. I told her the whole story and she told me that everything was going to be ok. I continued to walk to and from school, but with a group of kids. Safety in numbers is how my folks looked at it.

It was not long before I heard the words that we would be moving again. This time we were moving back east again. We were moving to Merrimack, New Hampshire. Only this time there would be something very different about the new house we were going to. Bob had an 18 year old daughter named Jackie. Jackie lived with Bob's ex-wife and she was too much for his ex-wife to handle. Jackie flew in to Phoenix, Arizona and, we picked her up to take her with us to Merrimack. I will never forget the first time I saw her. Being a boy at my age and due to my sexual dysfunctions, all I could do is stare at her large chest. I remember that she had the biggest well you know what I saying. She had a fowl mouth and, she smoked cigarettes constantly. It seemed like

Fire and Faith

every other word was the "f" bomb. She had a lot of silver rings on her

fingers, and she smelled weird. I don't think she liked me very much

judging by the way she looked at me. She was totally fake when she

talked to my mom. Jackie would kiss my mom's butt for everything

and, while my mother was not looking stole cigarettes from my

mother's purse.

Chapter 5

If I ever thought that the seven hour trip from Arizona to California was long, the trip back east took seven days. Once again Bob said I was not allowed to take my cat and this time he won. My grandmother agreed to keep the cat, so that when I visited her, the cat would be there for me. The trip back east was pretty much a blur. I slept most of the way there. We would stop at rest areas and my mother would go straight to work making lunches. While we would eat she would go and clean out the car in preparation for the next four hundred mile journey. The funny thing was that (with the exception of my mother being a Hebrew slave) we all got along pretty good. I think when you pile a bunch of people in a car and travel over two thousand miles in seven days; you tend to get "slap happy". All the little quarks are overlooked. It is just a shame that things could not have stayed that way.

When we got to the new place things started going downhill fast. There were plenty of arguments over petty crap. Bobs' main priority was to plug in the television so he would be able to watch the football game or, any other sporting event. Things went right back to the way they were. My mother in the kitchen and Bobs butt planted on the couch for the game. My new step-sister spent most of her time in her

Fire and Faith

bedroom except at dinner time. Dinner time was not any fun at all.
The only thing Jackie ever did was scream and yell at me about the way
I chewed my food. Sometimes I would argue with her, and Bob would
come to her defense. I was always (according to Bob) in the wrong.

One night at the dinner table, she was picking on me. Over and over
again she would pick and pick. I finally had enough and I stood up and
screamed at her at the top of my lungs. She immediately reached
across the table hitting me, and split my lip. Even then according to
Bob, I was at fault. I really hated living there. We lived in a rough part
of town, and I hated the new school. The only thing I enjoyed about it
was that they played marbles in the morning before class. I had always
played marbles. And not tooting my own horn, I was pretty good. It
was not long before Jackie started showing more of her true colors. My
mother's jewelry turned up missing, and Jackie knew nothing about it.
Jackie was into drugs, and was selling my mother's jewelry to keep her
supply of drugs coming in.

One day my mother and Bob went to see some friends, and I was
left alone with Jackie. For some reason or other she was being nice to
me, instead of beating me up. I went outside to shoot some hoops and
when I returned she was on the front porch smoking something. I was
only nine years old and not familiar with drugs of any kind. She asked

me to sit down with her. As I sat there watching her smoke and cough over and over again, my curiosity was building up. I don't think I really wanted to smoke it. I think I just wanted to be able to get along with her and, if that meant me smoking it, then I was going to. I finally said "What is it that you are smoking?" She handed to me and said, "Try it." I took a big hit off of it and just about choked to death. Right about that time my mother and Bob pulled up in the driveway. They did not catch us but, it was close. From that point on my step sister and I were friends. She had something on me and had something on her.

My mother's jewelry kept disappearing, and she finally got so mad that Bob had to take action. There was a massive fight in the house. Bob was yelling at Jackie, and my mother was yelling right along with them. My mother was in the kitchen when the fight broke out. I remember Jackie throwing a pot of boiling water at Bob. The fight continued for what seemed like hours to me, and it eventually moved into Jackie's bedroom. All three of them were screaming at the top of their lungs, and I needed to see what was going on. The house that we lived in had the old style doors with the key hole that you could look through. I ran from my bedroom down the hallway to Jackie's door to watch the excitement. I remember seeing her jump up off the bed with a fully closed fist and punching Bob straight in the face. He then came at her with his hands flying hitting her multiple times in the head. My mother did not know whose side to take. One minute she would say "Hey don't talk to your father that way" and, then yell "Hey Bob! Stop it! You're hurting her!"

I watched all the shoving, hitting and, screaming. It just would not end. For a brief moment I thought this was the greatest day of my life. I was not getting hit or yelled at this time. It was someone else. Every time it looked like it was coming to an end, Jackie would say something stupid, and it would start all over again. The fight finally came to an end as I ran back to my room and pretended to sleep. Jackie eventually moved out with her boyfriend, and started her own life. The funny thing about that episode (I probably should not say funny) but, she is currently serving a several-year term in a penitentiary. I guess she just could not stop stealing or, keep her mouth shut.

I used to have a friend there named Shane, and we were both into a song from Pink Floyd called "Another Brick in the Wall." We just had to have this album. One day we set out to go downtown with our bikes, and go buy this new album. On the way down there we had fun but, it was a long way. Unfortunately, the return trip was not as much fun. On our way back, we ran into some older kids carrying pipe wrenches. They wanted my bike and, they were not taking no for an answer.

Fire and Faith

Shane was safe because he took his sisters bike and, they did not want a pink girl's bike. There was a little scuffle and, I lost. They took all the parts off my bike. I ended up walking home with the bike frame in one hand and the new Pink Floyd album in the other, sporting a nice, fat lip.

When I came home, Bob was pretty mad at me as if it were my fault. He was upset that I did not beat them up. I explained that these kids had to have been sixteen or seventeen years old and, that I was only nine, not to mention that they had pipe-wrenches in their hands for weapons). Soon after, my mother put me in a karate class and, I was on my way to being a "full-fledged butt kicker". That did not happen either. I think I was in the class for about a month before I was taken out. I was taken out for good reason though, we were moving again. (I bet you didn't see that coming.) We were moving back to California. Once again, I was put on a plane to my grandmother house, and I was told that they would be there in a couple of weeks. Then we were going to go to California from there.

I was ten at that point, and on my way back to Arizona for two weeks during the summer. I was glad to see some familiar friends and, of course, my grandmother and grandfather. My grandfather was a craftsman. He could build anything and, he showed me the trade. To me, my grandfather was more than a craftsman. He was a true

Fire and Faith

definition of a man, father, grandfather and husband. I have often said that any worldly good in me, came from him. When I was a little boy, I got to stay at their house on rare occasions. My grandfather used to sit with me and draw Mickey Mouse pictures. He also used to play a game with me called pic-up-sticks. I would often think to myself that if I lived with them during my childhood years, I would have turned out fine. My grandfather's idea of discipline was a lot better as well. He did not believe in groundings and beatings. He would walk up, give you a swift kick in the butt and, tell you to get outside and play. I respected him enough when I was young to not get into trouble. He had a wonderful way of teaching a person a lesson using a calm voice, and displaying patience. He also believed that learning a good trade or skill was one of the most important things in life to learn. By the age of 15, I could build a house from the ground up. I really enjoyed hanging out with my grandfather.

My friends were important as well, and for the next two weeks, I surrounded myself with them. As the end of the trip grew near, I expected my mother to arrive from New Hampshire. I truly expected my somewhat stable life in Arizona to come to an end. I knew that Bob and my mother were on their way. One night just before I was getting ready to go to bed, my grandparents called me out to the living room.

Fire and Faith

They told me that my mother and Bob felt it would be better for me to stay with them indefinitely. It may not sound like a big deal, but to a ten year old child, it is abandonment. I felt like my mother did not want me around anymore, because it made it easier to get along with Bob.

When my grandparents told me, I tried to be tough and replied, "Its ok. I like it here." The truth was I wanted to be with my mother. I loved her, and wanted to be with her. The summer days passed by, and before I knew it, it was time to start school again. I thought for sure I would be attending school in Arizona. About two weeks before school started, my grandmother explained that I would be going to California to stay with my mother and Bob. She told me that she would be driving us there, and that we were going to be bringing my cat Tiger. It was a quick goodbye to my friends, because we left the next morning.

When we arrived in California, there was not much to do where they lived. My mother and Bob had chosen an apartment in a small town in Ramona, California. It was pretty much a rodeo town, and as a city kid, I did not fit in well. Needless to say, I did not like living there. I started school there and it took me forever to fit in. The kids were different than what I was used to. For some reason though, I found myself pretty good at football and so did the other kids. I remember

Fire and Faith

schools prior to this I used to have a fear of being picked last for any

the teams during P.E... At this time however that was not the case. I

was usually picked first, because I could run very fast and catch a ball.

In fact just about the time when I started to fit in, we were on the move

again.

I know at the time Bob was going to school to get his teaching

credentials. As for my mother she stayed at home while I was at

school. They decided to put me in boy scouts. That was okay I guess,

but still there was some strain there as well. Remember, I was a city

kid and really had no idea about camping, fishing, making knots, and

earning badges. Never the less I went to the functions and found them

to be rather boring. This time we moved because Bob could not find a

job. We had a neighbor that worked at a local grocery store, as a meat-

wrapper. She would bring us home steaks, ground beef and pork

chops. We had no money, but we had the best of the best when it came

to food. Bob used to say that "we were the richest poor people."

because of the great food.

We said our goodbyes to our neighbors and went back to Arizona.

It is a little fuzzy for me as to what took place next. I do know we went

back to California to the small town of Ontario. I actually liked this

town, and we actually stayed there for a couple of years. I made

Fire and Faith

friends quickly with the neighbor kids and life seemed pretty good for me. Living in the house however got much worse. It seemed to me that my relationship with my mother was growing more distant. Bob was slowly winning the battle for my mother's attention. And, of course, when I child does not get the attention they need, they start looking for bad attention. I started smoking at the age of eleven and smoking a little pot at as well. Bob's youngest daughter was sixteen, and she came to stay with us during this time. Her name was Karla.

Chapter 6

Karla and I got along great. In fact she was my saving grace with Bob. I started not caring about the good, warm, and fuzzy attention I wasn't getting from my mom anymore. I was wrapped up in swearing, smoking cigarettes, and the occasional pot smoking. Karla smoked cigarettes and pot, so things were great for me. Karla and I had each other's back. If she did something wrong I would try and cover for her.

I remember one night she came home really late. Our parents were out for the evening, and she planned on getting back before they did. I was sitting in the living room, when I saw the headlights from our car pull in the driveway. I knew it was not Karla, because her boyfriend would park down at the end of street. I quickly jumped up and ran to the bathroom and turned on the shower. When my parents walked in they asked where she was. I had told them that she was in the shower. It was late, and I knew my mother and Bob would go straight to bed without checking on her. Karla came home about a half an hour later. I went and turned the shower off and she made it to her room.

During the summer months she would send me to go and buy cigarettes at the local corner store. Karla would take the money from Bobs change jar he had hidden in his room. (Years ago all a person

Fire and Faith

needed was a note from a parent approving the cigarette purchase, if
you were under age.) This came at a cost to Karla though. She had to
give me half of the pack. This was a great deal for me because I always
had smokes. One weekend my mother decided to go and put my
laundry away, and she found three smokes on my dresser. I thought for
sure I was in trouble, but Karla had my back. She told our parents that
she had been in my room the night before and must have left them
there. Like I said we had each other's back. The problem was that
things started to get a little out of control with stealing the change...

Bob usually had about thirty to forty dollars in the change jar. One
night I heard Bob yell from the living room for Karla and me to come
see him. On the way down the hallway Karla asked me, "You got my
back right?" I remember walking out to the living room and seeing the
empty jar sitting on the coffee table. She had taken every dime of it. I
could not believe it. Bob said he wanted an answer to where the
change went. I immediately said "I did it." He said well then where is
it? I told him that I blew it on video games. I couldn't believe it, but
he bought the lie. The truth was Karla had stolen it to go to the river
with her friends the following day. I took a serious butt whipping on
top of being grounded for two weeks.

Fire and Faith

Karla felt as if she really needed to make it up to me. One night when our parents went out for the evening, we had a small party at the house. I had two of my friends over, and she had a couple of her really cute girlfriends over. I can't remember too much of that night, because I was pretty high. My motto used to be "if you can remember last weekend then you did not have a good time." What I do remember was that Karla had some really good weed, and I smoked a lot of it. The last thing I remember was sitting on the kitchen table eating a bag of cookies. Then I woke the next morning in bed. I had no idea how I got there. These kind of nights happened just about every time our parents went out.

Karla did not stay too much longer after that summer and ended up going back to Texas. After she left I started hanging out with a different type of friends and it was going great for a while. One of these friends lived on the other side of town. My mother had met him a couple of times but she did not like him. His name was Gregory. Gregory was a couple of years older than me. My mother had told me that I was not allowed to hang around him. But, I was not taking orders from her anymore.

One day I decided to walk all the way to Gregory's house. He lived in crappy apartment in South Ontario. Back in those days there were a

Fire and Faith

lot of Mexican gangs that ruled the area. I was graced in because I knew Gregory. When I got to his apartment, I could hear Gregory's mother yelling at him. Her language towards him was extremely foul, and his was to her as well. I did not even knock at the door before Gregory came out swearing at his mother over his shoulder. I asked him if he was ok and said "Yes, let go get some weed." This was normal for us and I agreed. We went to a different apartment complex which I had never been to. I asked where we were going and he said "It's cool, don't worry." Something just did not sit well with me. The one thing I had going for me, was my gut instinct. I still have it to this day. The problem was, I completely ignored it, and decided to go anyway.

I remember climbing the stairs to the second level, and my stomach just kept bugging me. I kept getting a cold flash across my forehead. As I walked up the stairs I tried to think of an excuse as to why we should not go to this apartment. It was about 2:00 p.m. and I was thinking I could use the "I am hungry" excuse. I asked Gregory if he was sure this guy was cool. He kept telling that everything was fine. He said we are going to score a little weed and then we would be on our way. Something still did not sit right with me, but I still went to the door. Gregory knocked at the door and there was no answer. He

Fire and Faith

knocked again only louder and harder, and yet no reply. I told Gregory

that he must not be home and that we should come back later. Gregory

said, "Hang on." as he banged on the door harder. At that moment a

man yelled from inside saying "Who is there? What do you want?!" I

could hear the man's heavy footsteps as he came closer to the door.

He opened the door fast and hard as looked out side to side to see

who was there. He was a large, fat man, and I immediately got the

chills as I flashed back to my old baby sitter. He had a zippo lighter in

his left hand, and he kept opening and closing the lid as he stared at

Gregory and me. I could smell something in the apartment that smelled

like trash, which had not been taken out in a few weeks. Finally, after

what seemed like ten minutes he said to come in. As we walked in, I

looked around and there was clutter everywhere. Every part of the

room had some type of decoration or some type of object piled up. The

place was cluttered beyond belief. Every part of the place had some

type of object or clutter.

As I looked around I had seen that he had a porno on the television

but the volume turned all the way down. To the left of me was the

dining room with a bunch of newspapers, and penthouse magazines on

the table. He told us to come into the dining room and sit down. As I

walked into the dining room I looked to the right of me to the kitchen.

this had to seem weird to my mother. I could hear Bob in the background telling my mother to get off the phone and help him. After she hung up, I could hear a dial tone, I said "You need me home now?" I said "ok" and hung up the phone. The fat man had the towel right there for me to clean myself up.

As I wiped away the filth, he kept saying that the next time he saw me he was going to take his zippo lighter and strike it across my ass. I think I was in shock because, I actually said to him, "I am not going to get pregnant am I?" I knew that boys did not get pregnant, but the words came out before I could stop them. He took the towel from me, and as he walking into the other room to put it away he said we were going to do it again. This was my only shot to get out. I ran as fast as I could with my shorts in my hand and made it out his door. I put my shorts on as I tried to make my way down the stairs. I did not even have my underwear; they were still in his room.

I was so scared; I kept looking over my shoulder on the way home. I had a long walk to get home. I had lost so much of myself back in that apartment. Actually so much was taken from me. The magnitude of pieces taken from me in both rapes was huge. I remember I kept thinking to myself, "I wish I was a normal boy. I wished I was just a kid. I was so ashamed of myself. I kept thinking "Why I didn't fight harder? Why didn't I at least fight? He was only a man, a man who feels pain like I do." I carried that feeling with me until I was in my late thirties. I remember I really wanted a cigarette, and I could not stop shaking. I could not stop myself from running, walking, running and walking. It was almost as if my body could not agree with my mind. I was either running or walking or indecisive.

By the time I hit the front door of my house I was somewhat calm. I could not get the feeling of his filth off the back of my legs though. When I came in through the door, Bob and my mother were putting up wall paper in the living room. They did not even look my way as went to my room. I got in the shower and scrubbed myself raw with a brush and soap. Even later that night I still had that sickening feeling of his body fluid on me. Once again I was feeling so hollow, like my brain or body was misplaced. I felt once again like a no body. I went to eat dinner after my shower, and the only words I heard from Bob was that I was grounded for two weeks for being five minutes late getting home. I was always being grounded for stupid things. When he told me that night that I was grounded I looked at him in disbelief, and as always, he mistook that for a dirty look. He added two more weeks to my grounding.

Fire and Faith

One of my ways of dealing with things that were bad, is I would tell myself over and over again that is was a bad dream. Most of the time this worked, but unfortunately I had to repeat this process over and over again for about a week. This was where my innocence for me was taken. I was robbed of my innocence with the first rape, but this one did the most damage. I never told my mother about what happened because I believed it was my own fault. As I look back I think that the rape was my tipping point of who I was about to become. I had a deep-rooted hate for fat men. I believed that they were all disgusting, and that all of them were child molesters. I remember Bob had a brother that would come by with his wife once in a while. She was a fat woman as well, and they must have weighed about 600 plus pounds combined. When he came to visit I would either stay in my room, or go outside. In fact all through my life up until I was in my early twenties I would avoid all fat men. As I got a little bigger and my attitude became a lot more dangerous, I knew that I would not be raped again. I almost wanted someone to try it so I could destroy them. I built up such a hatred for men that in the process I only wanted to be around girls. As far as I was concerned girls were soft and gentle and I could trust not to be hurt. My pain and distorted sexual behavior did not resurface until I was around fifteen years old, and stayed with me late into my thirties.

Chapter 7

During this time of my life I really wanted to be close to my father. (Like that was the right thing to do.) Strangely, no one could figure out why I wanted to have a relationship with him. My father had been a truck driver all of his life. He used to run what is called forty-eight states, meaning he drove all over the country. Somehow, my mother got in touch with him, and as it turned out, he lived in California as well. It seemed no matter where we lived my mother could find him. I would get to talk with him once in a while, and he made promises to me that the next time he came through my town, we would be able to see each other. I would be so excited to see him, yet he would never show up. This time however I thought it would be different.

I was older now, and I was not the crying little kid that he despised. When I talked to him on the phone he said he would meet me at the 76 truck stop. That truck stop was about five miles away, and I was not going to miss out on seeing him. I remember when the day finally came I was getting ready to meet him. I had asked Bob and my mother for a ride, and Bob immediately said "No." I must have had that look of confusion on my face or something, because he said that I was giving him a dirty look. Bob threatened that he was going to ground

Fire and Faith

me if I did not stop looking at him. I decided at that point that it would be best if I walked. It was a long walk but I made it. I was really hot and tired when I got there. I remember the waitresses at the truck stop were really nice to me. They sat me down, talked with me awhile, and gave me free sodas. (To a twelve year old boy, free sodas were great!). I must have waited a long time, because I woke up to my mother asking me if I was ready to come home.

The following weekend my father called and said he was going to make it to my house, and pick me up for the day. I was so excited and told my mother, and she asked me to give her the phone. I can still hear my mother telling him not to hurt me this time by not showing up. She also ripped him a new one for not showing the weekend before. I was so upset and afraid that he was not going to show after my mother yelled at him on the phone.

I remember being upset to the point that I started crying. Bob got up out of his chair and screamed at me "Stop being a baby! Stop crying over that stupid bastard." and that my father was a loser. Bob started putting my father down calling him horrible names. Bob just kept it up following me into every room in the house saying it over and over again, until I finally turned around and yelled back at him.

Fire and Faith

That is what Bob was waiting for. He told me even if my father did show that I would not be able to see him. That's all Bob ever wanted. It seemed like he was just trying to get me to fight with him. He was always antagonistic. My mother finally stepped in the middle of the argument and told Bob "Let him find out for himself if he is as bad as you say." The only thing I knew was that no matter what, I was going with or without the Bob's permission. When my father showed up though, things did not go according to my plan.

Bob was insistent on talking to my father. Bob was there to tell him all the bad things I had done since he'd known me. He told him all about my bad grades in school and that I had been caught several times smoking. My only thought was that he was going to ruin my chances of being able to see him. I thought to myself, "Why would my dad want to be with me now? He is going to hate me." I felt like I was falling apart, I started crying and wishing the day would just end. This went on for about an hour or so before my father said "Well, I better get going." I was so pissed off at Bob; he just ruined my time with my father. My father looked at me and said that he would see me the next time he was in town, which wasn't for a couple of weeks. As far as I was concerned, I figured with all the bad news that my father heard, he would never come back to see me.

Fire and Faith

A few weeks went by, and during this time I called him every weekend to see if he was home. He never answered the phone. I started to take it as he hated me because of what Bob said. It seemed about a month went by, and out of the blue my father called. He said that he was coming to pick me up, and take me to his house for the weekend, if it was ok with my mother. My mother agreed that it would be ok, and I went to go and pack my clothes. My father showed up a couple of hours later to pick me up. I made sure I was standing outside, so Bob would not talk to him. I could count on one thing, if Bob was on the couch he was not going to get up for anything or anyone. (In fact when I introduced my wife to Bob years later he did not even get out of the recliner he was lying in.)

My father showed up on time which was very surprising to me and my mother. He had a black, lifted Toyota 4X4 truck. This truck looked like a monster truck to me. In the back of his truck, he had two ATC's (All Terrain Cycles.) My father lived in Big Bear, California, and there were plenty of places to go riding. I was somewhat experienced as a rider. My mother and father talked for a short bit, while I was looking at the ATC's. Next thing I heard was a "Let's go." We got in the truck and we were on the road for the next two hours to his house. When we got into town we stopped at the local store and got

Fire and Faith

Coca Cola's, chips, and a box of Pop Tarts for me. We stopped at the video store and got a couple movies, and the last stop was at McDonalds for dinner.

When we got to his house it was close to dark, and I was ready to watch the movies. When we walked in the house he had a bunch of old photos at the table, as if he was recently going through them. I could see a couple of the pictures on top of the pile. They were of my mother and me when I was about four. There were a lot of pictures. I was not familiar with many of them. I could see what looked like military pictures. As I got closer I could see my father in uniform in one of the shots. My curiosity got the best of me, and finally asked him what the pictures were. He said that he had been going through some old things, and he came across this old box of photos. I am sure he knew what pictures were on the table. As he stood in the kitchen pouring the soda into the glasses, I continue my to let my fingers slide pictures around and take quick looks at each one.

As I made my way to the bottom of the pile I came across a picture with a man that was headless. The next photo showed the headless man's head on a fence post. I was stunned by the pictures, and could not come up with any words to say to my father. Everything seemed silent in the room while I was looking at these pictures. One picture

Fire and Faith

after another was of mutilated bodies of Vietnamese men. My father broke the deadly silence by saying "What do you got there?" He knew exactly what I had been looking at and, as calm as can be, he sat down at the table. He started telling me stories about how they used to drive trucks with barbed wire wrapped around the trailers. When they drove down the narrow roads at night in Vietnam, the Vietnamese people would be walking along side of the road, and would be torn to shreds. At the same time he would show me picture after picture of the dead bodies. I will never forget that night, and those images are forever burned into my memory.

We stayed up for a few more hours that night, watching the movies we had rented. I thank God that we watched comedies. It kind of helped numb my mind from the pictures I had seen. It was getting pretty late and we went off to bed. I knew we were going to be up early to go riding in the mountains. I could not sleep at all though. All I kept thinking about was the pictures of the dead people. I looked at my father in a whole new way. I saw what war could do to a man. It (war) could literally turn a man into a monster. Yet I still had a small spot of excitement about going riding the next day. My plan was to impress my father with my riding skills. I planned to show him that I could ride as good as he could. No matter what he did, I planned to do it just as well if not better than he could.

I woke to the smell of bacon and eggs the following morning. I jumped out of bed ready for the day. I came down stairs, and looked at the kitchen table. The pictures were not there. I noticed a small box labeled "Pictures for Joey." I was in no hurry to open that box. In fact I never did take that box of pictures home. We finished breakfast quickly, and made our way to the garage. As my father opened the garage door, the smell of gas and motor oil filled the air. To this day I love that smell. We topped off the fuel tanks on the ATC's, and we were on our way.

My father and I started out on a narrow dirt road just behind his mountain-top home. We started out the ride slowly until we were near the wider access roads. My father was in front of me. Occasionally he would look back to see if I was behind him and found I was right on his butt. I was determined not to fall behind. We climbed higher and higher up the mountain. We were going faster and faster up the mountain. I felt like I could make my move and I did.

I gave it full throttle and passed him. As I passed, I notice my father shaking his head back and forth but, it made no difference to me, I kept going. It took us about an hour and half to get to the top of the

Fire and Faith

mountain. My plan was to get to the top of the mountain first, having enough time to park, sit and, wait on him. I kept thinking he would be so impressed with me.

My plan worked. I made it there first. He didn't seem impressed with me; at least he did not show it anyway. We sat at the top of the mountain for a little bit before going down. I was tired after that serious ride to the top. I remember watching my father having a cigarette, and wanting one really bad. I got off the ATC for a little bit to stretch my legs before going back down the mountain. The view was beautiful with all pine trees and steep canyons. As I walked around I noticed my legs were a little shaky. I must have exerted a lot of energy hanging on to that bike on the way up.

I remember trying to take in as much oxygen as possible, but the thin mountain air made it difficult. I was used to living in the valley where the air was not as thin. My father asked if I was ready to go back down and not wanting to show weakness, I responded to with "Are you?" He kind of smiled and, started his bike up and made his way to the dirt road to head back down. I stood up as well, and started my bike. But it did not start right away. In fact it took multiple times to finally get it started.

Fire and Faith

My father had a pretty good lead on me so I had to make good time to catch him. I gave the ATC all it had, as I made my way down the curvy dirt road. Each turn was getting harder and harder to control but, I would not give up. I had to be getting close to him. I could see his dust-trail ahead of me. My body was starting to fatigue, and I could feel my arms begin to shake. As I would go into each turn, I found myself getting closer and closer to the edge of the mountain. I was not giving up though. I was so close to catching him! I was pushing way too hard, and something had to give.

As I came into the next turn, the left rear tire went off the edge. It was just enough for me to lose control. I remember looking to my left, and it was a long way down. There was nothing I could do. I was going over. I pushed myself off of the ATC but, in the wrong direction. Everything was moving in slow motion at this point. When I leaped, I found myself in front of the ATC. The only thing I could see was the tops of the massive pine trees. It was going to be a long fall down.

The first impact was somewhere between a thirty and fifty foot drop to the ground. The second impact was the ATC hitting me in the back which sent me flying in front of it again. The third impact was against a boulder about the size of a small car. The ATC at that point made contact with me again breaking my leg. When the ATC hit me the

Fire and Faith

second time it sent me flying again. When everything finally came to a
stop I was about eight hundred feet down. My ATC kept rolling down,
and rolled through someone's camp ground. In fact the people at the
campground eventually saw my father at the bottom of the mountain
and, asked him if he was riding with anyone else. They told him that
an ATC that looked just like his had just rolled through their camp-site.
He turned around and road back up the mountain to come find me.

I lay on the ground beat-up and broken. I could hear people, and the
faint noise of my father's ATC getting closer. I remember that I started
to yell for him, and it seemed like it took forever before he made it to
where I had gone off the road. My father yelled down to me, and asked
if I was ok. At that point the panic started to set in. The weird part was
that I was not feeling any pain. Even more strange, was that he never
came down to check on me. The only thing he did that was somewhat
kind was to offer me a cigarette. But, there was absolutely no way he
was going to get one down to me that far down in the ravine.

As I laid there in one position for what seemed like hours, I could
hear the faint noise of sirens. I tried to move my legs, but they were
not moving. I could not catch my breath, and my head was killing me.
The whole time I was down there, my father stayed silent, and never
made an attempt to get to me. I heard more from the campers below,

asking me if I was ok, and that the paramedics were on the way. They kept telling me to talk to them to stay awake.

I could hear the sirens getting closer and closer. I thought to myself, "Thank God I am going to be ok. The paramedics finally reached my father, and I could hear them ask my father what my name was. He told them that I was Joey. I heard in a loud voice "Joey, can you hear me?" I responded with panic and pain and "Yes." Then, I said to them, "Please don't leave me here!" Before I knew it they had made it to me. .

I remember they had all kinds of neat gadgets with them to work on me. One of the tools they had was this plastic bag that they put me in and then filled it with air, like a balloon. They told me that it would stop internal bleeding. Then they placed a wooden stretcher underneath me. The paramedics lifted me up and out. I remember saying "Please, don't drop me." Before I knew it, I was loaded into an ambulance and taken to the hospital. After being in the hospital for some time, I arrived back home.

I was stuck in bed for a while and kept wondering why I had not heard from my father. I tried to call over and over again. But, there was never an answer. I heard from my mother later that my father did not want to talk to me because he was mad that I wrecked his ATC.

Chapter 8

After a couple of weeks at home, I returned to school. During my time in school I was not a good student. I was more interested in girls as I approached puberty. For some reason I was always good with the prettiest girls in school. I am not bragging, but it was true. I was always able to date the most popular girls. But, my distorted view of sex made it a problem. The only thing I wanted to do was sleep with every girl I could. I dated a lot of girls in junior high school but, one really had my heart.

We would meet at the roller skating rink on Friday nights, go under the air hockey tables and just kiss. Everything about her was wonderful. I love the way she talked to me, and loved the way she laughed. Even when she was upset I loved the opportunity to talk her into happiness. But on those nights at the skating rink we would kiss for hours until we finally had to leave. This girl had my heart and, my time with her was growing short. My mother and Bob had been planning to move once again.

We would be moving a far-away to the high desert, and there would be no way for us to see each other. When this girl and I were not together we talked for hours on the phone. I would sneak out of bed at

Fire and Faith

night and lay on the kitchen floor with the phone. Back then I had to be careful not wake my parents. We had the old rotary phone hanging on the wall and it made a lot of noise when you dialed it. (Obviously I am a product of the 80s). We would talk all through the night.

The day we were moving was coming soon, and I remember getting a phone call from her telling me that we needed to break up. That was a devastating day for me. I don't know why I was so upset. It is not like we would be able to see each other. The following weekend came quickly, and we were loading our stuff in the moving truck. I remember looking out the window as we drove away. I was crying because I would not be able to see her again. I can still hear Bob telling me to "Shut up." He actually got so mad that he grounded me for two weeks.

When we finally made it to our new house, I could not wait to get out of the truck and get away from Bob. I hated him for moving us once again. The house we moved into was directly across the street from a church (Calvary Chapel). They enrolled me at the junior high school there in Hesperia, California. I did not adapt as well I had in the past starting a new school. I was really nervous and felt out of place. I immediately gravitated to the bad crowd, and quickly made a new kind of friends. These friends sat out on the football field at lunch time.

Fire and Faith

They smoked and drank liquor. My whole personality changed within a few weeks of being there. I started dressing all in black clothes. My favorite music was always hard rock, also known as heavy metal. But, it seemed to be getting harder. I felt like this new crowd accepted me for who I was without judgment. I could do or say anything I wanted, and they thought I was cool. I found I was accepted more by my friends than I was by my own family. Once again, I immediately started dating the prettiest girl in school and several others. Everything about me became focused on girls. School was my only social life because I was grounded most of time at home.

I hated being at home. It was not bad during the day because my mother and Bob were never at home. In fact, I looked forward to the times when my mother was without Bob. Even though we moved to Hesperia, my parents still worked in the valley. It was an hour commute, and they did not get home until at least six o'clock at night. This gave me plenty of time to get into trouble. I remember I was not allowed to listen to music. I am being very serious when I say that.

I used to have a small radio in my bedroom, and even that was eventually removed by Bob. Bob's idea of a bedroom was a bed and a dresser, and that was it. That was all I was allowed to have in my room. I remember one year my grandparents asked me what I wanted

Fire and Faith

for Christmas. I loved Christmas presents from my grandparents; they always got me what I wanted. For this particular Christmas I wanted a stereo with a bunch of albums including Black Sabbath, Ozzy Osbourne, Iron Maiden, Dio, Scorpions, and Motley Crue. I knew that if I asked for these items I would get them. There was not anything Bob could do about it. Bob used to get so upset with the gifts my grandparents got me, and my grandparents knew it. If I think about it now, I'm sure my grandparent's did it on purpose.

Both my mother and Bob worked for the school district, and they had a lot of time off during the year. At Christmas time they had two weeks off just like I did. This particular year we went to Arizona to visit my grandparents. I loved Christmas in Arizona. The smell in the air is unmistakable. The smell of every fireplace burning permeated the air. We arrived at my grandparent's house late in the day, and I was really excited to be there. Two things happened when we visited my grandparents. The first was that Bob could not be the normal jerk to me in front of my grandparents. Second, he could not be a jerk to my mother.

Christmas Eve arrived and I was excited about the next morning. My grandparents allowed me to open one present and then it was off to bed. I knew Santa Clause did not exist anymore. My mother one year

Fire and Faith

(by mistake) put the Santa gifts under the tree one week early, and that was when I figured it out. There was no big disappointment to me though. I just realized that my mother did even more for me. I was so excited for the following Christmas morning that I had a very difficult time sleeping. I think it was about 5:30 in the morning, and I was awake. I couldn't take it anymore. The excitement was overwhelming. I ran from my bedroom down the hallway, and to my surprise as I came around the corner to the living room, the whole room was a golden color. The lights on the tree were beautiful. They sparkled and twinkled like they had their own melody. There were many gifts wrapped in beautiful colors. It was like I was looking at a magazine. I imagined if there was a Santa Claus, his home would look much like this one.

I've always shown favoritism in opening the Christmas stockings. At my family's house, the stocking seemed to be the most fun, and was always the first gift we would open. I remember reaching for my stocking that was placed on a hook over the fireplace. As I sat down on the overstuffed couch, I could hear that others in the house were getting up. I reach in and grabbed the first little gift. I gave a slight shake and heard that whatever it is was rather hard. My grandpa used to joke and say that if I did not behave, that Santa Clause would only bring me

Fire and Faith

coal. When I opened it up I found a small red tin. Inside the tin were about 9 small pieces of coal. (I still have that tin to this day and, some years I played the same joke on my daughters.)

As I set the coal aside and got ready for the next gift inside my stocking, Bob walked out and said, "You wait for everyone else." He was changing tradition! I was a little upset with this. Right about that point my mother and grandmother came out to the living room and asked, "Have you opened your stocking yet"? I guess I must have had an upset look on my face because at that point Bob said; "Now you can wait until everyone has had their showers and coffee before you open anything." My grandmother and mother said "You can't make the boy wait that long!" Bob stuck to his word and I waited until everyone was done. I don't think I really cared because, I knew the rest of the morning was going to be fun.

I remember my grandmother said, "Go ahead and open the smaller ones first." The first thing I opened was the Ozzy Osbourne album Diary of a Madman. Bob was so mad that I was given anything to do with rock music. I was so excited and noticed that there were probably at least ten more wrapped the same way. This meant that I got every album that was on my list. The only problem that I saw was how I was going to play them. I really did not want to have to leave them there and only play them when I visited. But, I remembered there were several large gifts yet to be opened. I kept ripping and tearing them open, and finally came to the last big gift. In all honesty, I had no idea what it was, due to the odd shaped box. It was big, but I could not figure out what it was.

My mother and I have a rare talent when it comes to gifts. We have the ability to shake the box, and know exactly what it is. So my family got smart and started putting the gifts in different boxes with other items such as socks, or whatever else would take up the room. I assumed that was that they had done, due to the size of the box. My mother and Bob were sharing their own gifts, and were not paying attention to what I was doing. I ripped into this large package and discovered it was a stereo. I could now play all the albums I just got! Bob looked my direction when I yelled displaying my excitement. I remember him telling me in a stern voice, "Joey, settle yourself down!" My excited smile turned into sadness. Bob said "There is no way you are taking those gifts home." He actually got up, and was so mad that he left the room. I was saddened to think that I could not take the gifts home, that the next thing I did was to go to the kitchen and steal a cigarette from my mother's pack. I went to bathroom, opened the window and smoked it. When I came out of the bathroom they had all been arguing. My mother and grandparents won. I would be taking my stuff home.

The trip back to California was long and miserable. Bob could not stop talking about how horrible my grandparents were, and how they had gone against what he said. When we finally got home, I could not wait to set up my stereo, and play all the cool records. As far as I was concerned, I never had to leave my room again. After I set the stereo up I started playing them. I probably had the music on for about ten minutes when Bob walked into my room, and told me to "Turn it down." It was barely loud as it was. The house we lived in was really big. Bob and my mother had built an addition on the house, and it was all the way on the other side of the house. That is where the television was, and they were there all the time. If I had my stereo on volume level six, you could not hear it from where they were sitting. Bob would walk down the hallway, passing my room on the way to the bathroom, and that is when he could hear it. So Bob would come in say that he could hear it, and I had to turn it down. He totally robbed the fun out of everything. (I have three daughters, and when you stand in my living room you can hear all three stereos playing different music. My wife and I believe that music is more important than television.)

Fire and Faith

The only time I could really crank up the stereo was when Bob and my mother were gone. As I mentioned before we lived across the street from a church. The church service on Wednesdays always got a dose of Black Sabbath, and other types of loud rock and roll. The music could not be heard in the church, but the people in the parking lot got to hear it. I know now that probably was not the coolest thing to do. I remember someone from the church came over to tell Bob about what I'd been doing, and that was the last time I was able to play my records. Bob did not do anything about it that day. However I did go to a friend's house that next Saturday, and when I came home my stereo was mysteriously broken. Bob had "no idea" how it happened. The record player was somehow broken. He in fact actually blamed me for it. He told me that I was so rough on everything that it had to be my fault. I remember I actually asked him if he did it, and he flipped out on me. He was so angry that he was screaming at me. He actually came at me swinging.

My mother was on the other side of the house when she seen this happen. I could see over Bobs shoulder and my mother was running to get in the middle of us. My mother was telling Bob to stop it, as he was swinging his arms over my mother trying to hit me. I remember him yelling I don't want his ass here anymore. I want the kid out now!

Fire and Faith

My mother kept saying to him "where is he going to go, he is 14!" Bob did not care he wanted me out of the house. He finally walked away saying he hated me. She turned to me and said "go to bed, and that we would talk in the morning."

The next morning came and I was not looking forward to one of Bobs lectures. His lectures went for hours. During these lectures, I was not allowed to talk; only Bob or my mother could speak. These lectures would be so long that when I looked at Bob I would not blink, it was kind of a game I would play. I would stare for so long the room would start to darken and eventually look black. I would blink and the room would become bright again and then I would repeat this process over and over again. Sometimes I would stare for so long his face looked like it was mutating. If I did try and communicate, Bob would say I was being rude or tell me to stop giving him dirty looks and he would ground me. There were times that some lectures cost me 2 months of grounding, because I tried to speak. This is why I later in life had a hard time communicating. I simply did not know how to share my feeling in a positive way. Most of the time I would blow up with the smallest things instead of dealing with what was really bothering me. This lecture was no different. I ended up being grounded for a month and half. I was so sick of Bob I was really starting to hate him. Everything in my room was removed once again, except my bed and dresser.

I used to sneak outside once in a while and smoke a cigarette around the corner of our garage. One day it was just before dinner and I was outside trying to have a smoke. It was really windy outside and it was hard for me to light it. So I turned around the corner and struck a match just inside the garage door. The smoke finally lit and turned back to get behind the garage wall, and when I did Bob was right there. He scared the crap out of me, not because I was smoking but because he was right there.

Bob grabbed me and dragged me into the house. I would have walked but he was so forceful I could not get my feet underneath myself to actually walk. He dragged me through the door into the kitchen. My mother was freaking out yelling, "what is going on!" Bob said, "I caught this little bastard outside having a smoke!" He screamed at me saying, "You like smoking?" He said: well then guess what you are having for dinner?" Bob made his way to the top of the refrigerator where kept his cigarettes, and grabbed a pack and open them up. He was so enraged, and he took a cigarette out and jammed in my mouth. One after another he made me eat the cigarettes. I did not eat the whole pack, but I did eat about 10 and that was enough for me

Fire and Faith

to be sick. He told go to my room and that he would be back. There were times I was so angry and I was so hurt I wanted to actually shoot myself. As I mentioned before Bob had guns, and sometimes when they were not home, I would get one of them and sit on the couch. I would unload the revolver and put it to my head and pull the trigger. Sometimes just before pulling the trigger, I would think to myself if I got all the bullets out.

While I was in my room, I could hear Bob arguing with my mother. She said that he was out of line. They argued for a longtime, and then I heard Bob say while he was down the hallway, "I am going in there to kick his ass." I immediately looked around, like I was going to hide or something. He came through my bedroom door and I was on my bed all the way against the head board. He yelled, "Get up!" I started to get up and when I did he punched me straight in the face. I tried to go around the other side of my bed and get out my door, but he was already there. He swung at me again and missed. I pushed him with all my might and fell through the closet door. I was in shock, "I just pushed him down." I just stood there, and he got back to his feet. He reached out and grabbed my shirt and punched me again. When I fell back he still had a hold of my t-shirt and ripped from the collar down. He stood over me and challenged me to get up. I was no fool; I was not

98

getting back up. Bob said to me "get yourself cleaned up and meet me in the backyard."

He walked out of my room and I stayed in there for about five minutes, debating whether or not I should just run away. I found the courage to go out back so I made my way down the hallway and into the living room. I will never forget what I saw out the sliding glass door. My mother and Bob were sitting on the picnic table in the backyard with their back to me. My mother had her arm around him scratching his back and hugging him. She was out there consoling him while he acted like he was the hurt one. I couldn't believe I was so mad at the both of them. As he was sitting outside with my mother, I remember standing behind them swinging and throwing punches towards the door as if I was actually hitting them. I remember swearing at him and saying you will never hit me again. They could not hear or see me, but it made me feel a little better I guess. All in all I just wanted to leave.

I slid the door open to the backyard and my mother just looked at me while she rubbed Bobs back. Bob asked me if I saw the shovel that was against the wall. He said get that shovel and start digging. When I picked that shovel up, I thought to myself, "I should just hit him with it." Instead I replied to him and said with a shaky voice "what am I going to dig?" He told me to pick a spot and start digging a 4 foot hole. The hole had to be 4ft. wide by 4ft. long and 4ft. deep. After I dug the first hole I asked him what next? He said fill it in and start another one, and keep going for the rest of my vacation. I think that I dug the whole property which was about a half-acre. Maybe I didn't, but there was a lot dug.

The rest of the Christmas vacation finally ended, and I was going back to school; finally freedom from the house. I returned back to school on that Monday and I could not wait until lunch. I knew I would be able to go out onto the football field with all my friends. As we walked toward the football field I lit up a cigarette. Normally I would do this further out on the field and I should have waited. I was seen by a teacher and was brought to the office. The punishment was quick, and I was expelled. My grades were so poor and I had been in trouble before with the school, and I just figured that it would best that I did not come back. Bob and my mother were so upset that this had happened.

Of course there was a big lecture on top being grounded. I remember that at the end of the lecture Bob told me to go and get a shower and go straight to bed. The anger was building in me and when I got in the shower, I started saying everything that I wanted to say

Fire and Faith

during his lecture. I apparently said it loud enough for Bob to hear me.

Bob came through the bathroom door and swung the curtain wide open.

He was yelling at me asking me if I was a "tough guy." He was

punching me through the shower curtain, and yelling. He said this over

and over again until I finally responded by saying "no." Bob said that's

what I thought, and at that moment he looked down at my genitals and

said "you little prick!" To be truthful, those words echoed in my head

until I was in my mid-30s. I actually had a complex for years. That is

the one of the things I refused to do to my children and that is name

calling. I believe it takes so much away from the child.

My mother enrolled me into a new school that following day. This

was the school that all the trouble makers attended. I really did not

want to go to this school. I have moved around so much that with each

move I would get more and more scared each time. In fact for some

reason I really hated this school, and I knew how I was going to get

kicked out. The funny thing is when you are a kid; you really don't

think things through. I walked down hallway in between classes and lit

up a cigarette. Everyone thought I was crazy and yet I felt cool doing

it. What a way to rebel. I think I probably took three drags off of it

before I was caught. The thing about this school was if you screwed up

once you were immediately kicked out. This was called hook

elementary and it was kind of like the last stop. If you screwed up there, then that was pretty much the end of school for a person. The next step was a different district.

They called my mother and she came to get me. Bob was not home yet from work, so it was just my mother and I at home. She started asking me what was wrong. When I started to let things out about how I hated Bob, my emotions got away from me. I started yelling and crying, and she started to yell back at me. At one point it got so intense that my mother was going to swing at me and I lifted my arm. Not to hit her but it was reflex to block what was about to come. She walked away from and left me standing in the living room. My mother went straight for the phone and called my grandparents.

I can still here how the conversation went. She told them that she thought I was going to hit her, and that she had seen it in my eyes. She told them that she wanted me to go and stay with them. When I heard her say that I thought, I can't believe that she was going to send me away again. Once again I did not matter enough to her. The problem was no one would listen. Just because I got into trouble did not mean I was a bad kid. The problem was everyone was only paying attention to the things I did wrong, rather than actually listening to why I was acting out. Kids do not know how to express their feelings most of the time, especially under the circumstances I was in. She told them that I would have to be enrolled in school there to finish the year. I think there were only about two and a half months left of school.

Bob came home that night and I was in my room. I got close to my bedroom door to listen to what was being said. My mother told Bob what had happened and I heard Bob say "I am going in there to kick his ass!" My mother pleaded with him not to do that. She said that I was being shipped to my grandparents' house to live there. I heard Bob say "Good I don't want that kid here." Later that evening my grandparents called the house and asked to speak with me. When I got on the phone they asked me if I wanted to go out there to live; like I really had a choice. At the time, even though I hated Bob, I thought I hated my mother for shipping me off. I don't think I really hated my mother, I think the disappointment was confused with hate. My grandparents at the time, asked what I thought about being adopted by them, and that we would talk about it more when I got there.

Chapter 9

My grandmother came out to California to pick me up and bring me back to Arizona. I had everything packed and ready to go. I did not have much, but a few records that I got for Christmas and a broken stereo. My goodbyes to my mother and Bob were quick and before I knew it, we were on the road. As we drove down the road we came to the corner store. My grandmother said she was going to get gas and some snacks for the road. I decided to wait in the car and listen to the radio. When my grandmother came out of the store she had a small bag of snacks and soda for me to drink. I looked through the bag of goodies and noticed a pack of cigarettes that happened to be my brand. I asked my grandmother when she started smoking this brand of cigarettes. She said that they were mine to have, because she did not want me to be stealing hers. The trip was actually an enjoyable one, and we talked all the way back to Arizona. I explained to her what had been going on, but I would never talk about the heart of my problems. Number one, I did not want to show my shame, and number two I did not know how to truly communicate. I always felt that if I said what I felt I would be shipped away, or somehow belittled.

Fire and Faith

When we got to Arizona it was hot. I did not care though. I was too excited to be there with my grandparents. I often think if I was there to begin with instead of going through all the crap, I would have turned a lot different. The problem with that though, is I would not be writing this book. I still had the weekend before I had to start school. My grandmother thought it would be a good time to go clothes shopping for the remainder of the school year. We went on a long shopping spree. I was able to get clothes that I liked. She was a little old fashioned, but in the end I got the clothes I wanted. I was interested in concert t-shirts and Levi 501's. We did not stop there though. She felt it was important for me to be able to have my bedroom the way I wanted it. We got posters of my favorite rock bands, and the music magazines that I enjoyed reading. She also got me a new stereo for my room. That was so awesome to me because I hadn't been able to hear the records that I had in a long time. I really wanted to be a musician when I grew up, and I shared that with my grandmother. She asked me what instrument I wanted to play, and I quickly told her that I wanted to play guitar. She told me that if I did well for the rest of the school year, she would buy my guitar.

Monday came quickly, and my grandmother and I went to enroll me in school. I was finishing my ninth grade year. When I started school,

Fire and Faith

I quickly met a friend that was into the same kind of music as me. We planned to start a band together, and make it to the "big time". We had dreams of going on tour, partying, and playing music for the rest of our lives. During this time I met my first love. Her name was Sandy. I met her right at the end of the school year. I remember she was signing my yearbook, and she wrote her phone number in it saying "Call me." A few days later, school ended officially marking the beginning of summer. I did not know it yet, but I was about to go through a serious change.

Sandy and I were together all the time. I stopped hanging out with my best friend. As far as I was concerned, Sandy was the center of the universe. When we were together we always kissed and touched each other. We could not wait to be alone. Each time we were together, we would go a little further with the touching. I did not take long before we started removing each other's clothes, and going all the way. We had sex for the first time when I was 15. It was my first time, but it was not her first time. This was the best feeling in the world to me. Every time we were together I would find a private area so we could have sex. It did not matter where we were. She was brave as far as public sex, and so was I. Sandy and I were not in front of people, but we were in public areas. I think it added more intensity to our time together. Our time was short together before I heard the dreaded words from my grandmother. My grandmother told me that my mother and Bob were driving back east to visit Bob's family. My grandmother agreed to drive back there as well to visit her own family. We would be driving in separate cars and I agreed to go as long as I did not have to be with Bob and my mother. I was so sad that I had to leave Sandy, but I promised that I would write and get her gifts along the way.

—The day Bob and my mother arrived to my grandparents' house came too quickly. When Bob and my mother came into the backyard they found me in the pool. I was excited to see my mother, but there was no excitement to see Bob. He was acting like his arrogant self and I wanted no part of it. I got out of the pool and dried myself off and lit up a cigarette. I did not do this on purpose to piss Bob off. I just was used to being able to smoke when I wanted. He was so mad at me being allowed to smoke that he just walked away. I spent the rest of the day on the phone with Sandy. We talked about how great it was going to be when I came back, and we were together again. Saying goodbye to her seemed like the world was going to end for me. I finally went off to bed. I remember that I could not sleep. I really did not want to leave the one thing that I loved beyond anything. The night lasted forever.

Fire and Faith

I woke up to my mother coming in and jumping on my bed and tickling me. My mother used to do that on occasion. I also remember that when she and I would sometimes go to the grocery store, she would grab my hand, and swing it back and forth really high. I would act like she was embarrassing me, but inside I loved every bit of the attention. As I started to wake up, she told me that she and Bob were leaving right then, and that Grammy and I would be leaving later. She gave me a big kiss and told me she loved me. She also said that we would meet up in a couple of weeks at the campground that they were going to be staying at. I got up out of bed and walked my mother to the car, and we said our goodbyes. As I watched my mother drive away, I realized at that point how much I loved and missed her.

It was a little later in the day and my grandmother and I finally left to go. It took almost two full weeks to get back to the east coast. My grandmother and I took our time getting back there, and we had a great time together. Along the way I visited my two cousins that I had not seen since I was about six. It was a great time. I knew that the trip was not going to be good for too much longer. We would meet up with Bob and my mother soon. They were staying at a campground by a lake. My grandmother was going to drop me off there, and go visit some of her friends that were further away. All of Bob's family was there. I

Fire and Faith

did not know these people at all. The one thing I did know was that Bob had a step sister named Donna.

Donna had several kids, but she also had a daughter my age. Her name was Cindy, and this girl was beautiful. She was really different from Sandy. We immediately gravitated to each other. At the campground we were staying at there were a lot of different activities. One of the upcoming activities was going to be a dance. I did not see the harm in asking Cindy to the dance. I mean let's be serious, her mother was not blood related to Bob. Bob and Cindy's mother were step brother and sister, and Bob was my step dad. It is not like the family tree would grow straight up. It was just a dance. I asked Cindy to the dance, and she thought it was a great idea. The next couple of days before the dance we were together the whole time. We would leave the rest of the family, and stay out in the woods and just talk. We would kiss now and then, but it was nothing serious. She had a boyfriend at home, and of course I had Sandy waiting in Arizona, or so I thought.

The day of the dance finally arrived. The dance did not start until early evening, so we had the whole day just hang around together. We ended up walking around to the other side of the lake and found some old picnic tables to sit down at. I remember she was sitting Indian style

Fire and Faith

on top of the table, and I was lying down with my head on her lap. Believe it or not, that was about as close as we got with our bodies. Cindy and I stayed there for a couple of hours. We decided to head back to camp where the rest of the family was. We also figured it was time for us to get ready for the dance. As we got closer to the campsite, the other kids ran to our parents yelling "They're back! They're back!" Right about that time Bob came around the camp trailer, and grabbed me by my neck. He never said a word while dragged me into the camp trailer.

I remember seeing the whole family was staring at me, and I was humiliated. Bob started drilling me about what I was doing with Cindy. He thought that we were off having sex in the woods. I kept thinking to myself that I probably should have, so I could at least feel better about the trouble I was in. He told me that I was to never go near her again, and that I had to stay in the trailer for the rest of the vacation, that was two weeks. My mother tried once again to change his mind, but that did not happen. My mother always tried but never actually laid down the law. I pleaded to go to the dance, but I was told that I had to stay in the trailer. The memory remains stuck in my mind that when everyone left the campsite I was stuck in the trailer.

Fire and Faith

Off in the distance I could hear the music. Everyone was laughing and having a great time. The longer I sat there, the more and more upset that I became. I finally decided that I was not going to stay in trailer anymore. I was going to go use a pay phone, and call my grandmother to find out how long it would be before she would be back to pick me up. Bob had taken my cigarettes earlier in the week, and told me that I was not allowed to smoke. So in return, before I left to go use the phone, I took my smokes back. I found them in his suitcase, and lit one on the way down to the payphone. When I tried calling my grandmother there was no answer. As I turned around to head back to the trailer, Bob was standing right there. It is as if he was waiting for me to leave the trailer.

Once again, he grabbed me by the back of my hair, and dragged me all the way back to the trailer. Along the way it was really starting to hurt, so I was reaching for his hand to make him stop. Each time I did this he kept telling me, "Come on!" As we got closer the pain was at a final peak for me. Finally, I swatted at his hand, and yelled "Let me go!" I remember he spun around and basically challenged me to a fight. He started to shove me around, then reached around and grabbed my hair again heading back to the trailer. I wanted to hit him so bad. I wanted to beat that man. I knew that I would not win though. I

Fire and Faith

honestly believed I was going to have to stay in that five foot by six

foot trailer for next two weeks, but that did not happen. The following

morning my parents got a message that there house in California had

been vandalized. My mother and Bob hired some older boys to house

sit while my they went on vacation. I remember my mother coming in

that morning waking me up and saying that we had to pack and leave

immediately. I told my mother to get a hold of Grammy to come pick

me up. My mother said that she was not due back for another week or

so, and that I had to go with them. I asked her how I was going to get

back to Arizona, and she said that they would drive me out later.

We were on the way back to California within two hours of getting

notice about the house. The trip was long. Bob and I fought and argued

all the way back to California. I just wanted to go back to my

grandparents' house. It took four days to get to California. The house

was not as bad as described. But it was horrible to my mom and Bob.

I just did not care if the house burned down. There was still a little

over two months left of summer. Bob and my mother came to me and

told me that I would not be returning to Arizona. They were going to

take me to Texas to visit my step sister Karla, Bob's daughter. Once

we were on the road and half way to Texas, my mother and Bob told

me that it was not just a visit. They were taking me there to live with

Fire and Faith

Karla permanently. I was not happy with this decision. I liked Karla, but I did not want to live with her or live there. I could not believe they tricked me to get me there. I could not figure out why I just could not be with my mother. That is what hurt the most.

Once we got to Texas, Bob and my mother were only there for one night before they left. I was told I had to find a job while I lived there, so I could pay a little rent to Karla and her husband. My first job was working with her neighbor. Karla's neighbor hired and fired me within two weeks. The problem he had with me was that I couldn't get to work on time. The reason why I could not be on time was because I was always getting high. Karla was a big time user of drugs, and I was allowed to have whatever I wanted there. I was smoking weed, drinking beer and for the first time used cocaine at fifteen years old. Every night was the same at Karla's. I was always high and drunk. I had to have a job though, so I took a job working construction for a guy who owned his own small business. That lasted for about month or two, before him and I did not get along. I was not experienced and he was frustrated. Then I got another job working in a fast food restaurant. That only lasted about three weeks, because I was fired for hitting and knocking out my boss. Two things came out of beating my boss up. The first was the realization that I could beat a full grown man.

Fire and Faith

(I knew at that point, Bob was not going to be a problem for me anymore.) The second thing was that I was not allowed to live with Karla anymore. Karla's husband said "No job. No place to stay." I was put on a bus and sent back to California.

The twenty-four hour trip was miserable. Half of my belongings were stolen while I slept on the bus. When I got back to California my mother was there alone to pick me up. I was so happy to see that Bob did not come with her. I knew there was a problem though, and I knew I was not going to be able to stay with her in California. Summer was coming to an end, and I did not have much time before school started. I asked my mother if she was going to enroll me when we got back. She told me that I was not going to be able to stay with them and that I had to go back to my grandparents' house. I had known deep-down that was going to happen. My mother also said that I would be leaving the next day. I had just enough time to get something to eat, shower and sleep for about 8 hours before I had to leave again. There was good news combined in all of the bad. I would get to see Sandy again and we would be back together. I stayed in touch with her the whole summer with the exception of when I was in Texas for that short time.

By the time we got back to Arizona I had to start school the following Monday, because Arizona starts much earlier than California.

Fire and Faith

I was really excited. I tried to get a hold of Sandy all weekend, but she never seemed to be home. The weekend passed quickly. I was so ready to start my first day at school. I wasn't able to go straight to my classes, because my grandmother had to take me into the office for my new schedule. I was bummed because I really wanted some of same the classes as Sandy. After getting my schedule, I was a little late to my first class. When I walked into the first class, I saw my best friend from the previous year. I sat right next to him and tried to talk to him, but it almost seemed like he was ignoring me. I was not too concerned because I knew I was going to see Sandy right after that class.

The bell finally rang, and I was on my way to the locker area, I knew for sure I would see her there. Just as I was getting ready to leave the class the teacher asked me to stay back just for a minute. The teacher looked over my schedule and then sent me on my way. As I walked out the door, I saw Sandy with my best friend. My whole world, (at least what was left of it) fell apart as I watched them walk right past me. They did not even see me, I could not believe it. This was the girl that I lost my virginity to, and she just stepped on me like I was nothing. I went up to both of them and asked what was going on. Sandy said I had been gone for too long. I always thought that this would be a good excuse if we never talked. But we stayed in touch all

Fire and Faith

summer. I figured the next thing I had to do was to get Sandy back.

What I didn't understand was the combination of the sexual abuse as a

child, and my sexual activity with Sandy was leading to a totally

different road than I had been on. My perspective on sex was not good

at this point, at all. I also know now, that I should not have had sex at

all during these early years.

The first move I made was to target Sandy's best friend. She was

very cute, and I was determined to be with her. In fact, over the next

five months I had sexual relations with sixteen different girls. It started

with Sandy's best friend. I did not know it at the time, but she was a

virgin. I was with her for about a month before having sex. During

this time I also was with two other girls. I had no respect for any of the

girls. Don't get me wrong; in my mind I loved every one of them, and

some I feel I truly did love, but others were pure lust. I found it so

fulfilling that these girls liked me enough to have sex with me. To me

it was like being loved by a lot of people. If I could only go back in

time and undo everything, I would. To this day, I am ashamed that I

hurt so many girls. (Today, I have forgiven myself to the best of my

ability.) I still have yet to apologize to all of those girls for my actions

simply because I have no idea where they are today. In fact if there is

anyone reading this book that I have wronged, please let me apologize

Fire and Faith

to you now by saying "I am sorry for being the person I was back then, and it was not my intention to hurt anyone."

Chapter 10

During this time my father had contacted me, and we'd been talking on the phone. Somewhere along the line, someone thought it would be best that I go and stay with him for a while. This move may have been initiated by me, but my memory is a little unclear. Nevertheless, I ended up moving to North Carolina where my father lived. My father had re-married a woman that I thought was pretty nice. I flew to North Carolina on a Saturday and started a new school Monday. I really did not want to start a new school, but I could not stay home either. Let me describe a little about what I looked like. I was about five foot, eleven inches tall and really skinny. I had really long hair, and I loved hard rock music. I had just moved to Waynesville North Carolina. Right off the bat, this was a bad mix. The boys back there loved country music and wore cowboy hats and cowboy boots. Needless to say, my different appearance made me very popular with the girls, but the guys hated me.

I went to the mall at one point with the only guy that would hang out with me. He was the only guy that like the same music I did. He was full of questions about California, and always said that one day he was going there to be a rock star. As we were leaving the mall there was a pick-up truck in the parking lot. In the back of the truck there were seven big football players drinking beer. I knew there would be trouble. I just kept my head down and walked at a quick good pace to get past them. It did not matter though. They started in with the long hair jokes, and calling me a pretty girl. This kept up as we walked by and, finally one of them threw a beer can at me and that was it. I'd had enough! I turned around and yelled at them saying "Come on! Who's first?" The bigger problem was that they all jumped out. The only thing I could think to do was to hit the biggest one there. So I did just that. I hit him with everything I had in me. I hit him again and again. I thought to myself, "I am doing it! I am winning!" I forgot about the other six boys though. They decided to join in, and they beat the crap out of me. I remember going down, and then I saw nothing but their feet. They kicked me over and over again. When it finally ended I looked around for my friend. As I looked up, he came rushing up in car slamming on the brakes. He jumped out, pulled me into the car and took me his house.

My father was still driving trucks, and it was rare when I actually saw him. I think he was home every other weekend but it was only two days. Realistically, by the time he got home and prepared to leave again, it was only one day. He would get in about 2:30 a.m., and sleep

Fire and Faith

until about 9:00 a.m. He would spend that one day at home and then leave that next morning at 6:00 a.m... When he was home, there was really no conversation between us. In fact, it was like old times. I stayed in my room most of the time, while he and wife hung out together. The attention that I lacked from him eventually showed up in my behavior. My father and his wife went away for a weekend and left me at home alone. I was told that I was not allowed to ride the ATC's while he was away. I don't know if what I planned to do was considered a normal boy's mischief, or a cry for a father's attention. Either way it did not matter at the time. The truth is though I often think about if that was just normal or problematic? Meaning I hear about kids today that stole their mom's car at night and went out joy riding, so to me this was no different.

I took the ATC out one day, not expecting my father to return until the following day. When I came home after a long ride, I saw my father's truck in the driveway. I knew I was caught and there was no getting out of it. I parked the ATC in the garage, and I waited there for a while. I sat alone trying to think about what I was going to say. When I lifted the garage door I saw my father sitting on the stairs that lead to the house. I stood there frozen. I had no idea what to say. The only words the came out of my mouth was "I am sorry." I will never forget the way he looked at me. He looked at me with absolute disgust and said "You blew it kid." Then, he poured his coffee on the ground, stood up, went up the stairs and into the house. They must have come home really early, because I found a plane ticket sitting on my bed when I went into the house. I did not even have to time to pack anything, I was leaving right then. I had to leave all my belongings behind. They would be shipped to me at a later time.

I was on the plane back to California by 8:00 o'clock that night. When I arrived at the Ontario airport in California, there was no one there to get me. I thought at least my mother would be there, but there was no one. I grabbed my suitcase and sat outside at the curb. I was probably outside for about forty-five minutes when my mother showed up. She told me that my father never even called to say that I was on the plane. I guess my father decided to call after my plane landed. What a fine way to get me back for taking the ATC out. My mother and I were on the road back to Hesperia, California. It was about an hour ride from the airport. The ride was nearly silent except for when she asked if I was hungry. The whole ride home I just kept thinking that I was not welcome in my mother's house. I knew Bob hated me and I hated him as well. When we arrived, the first thing Bob said to me was "You screwed that up too, huh?" I did not even want to fight with him. I just wanted to lie down. I was really tired from the six hour flight, and worse, emotionally drained from what just happened with my father. I always felt like a failure with everything I did.

I must have been pretty tired because I slept the whole day until dinner time. My mother woke me up and asked if I wanted dinner and I said yes. When we sat down at the dinner table Bob asked me if there was any place I could go and stay. I thought he was joking, I mean come on I was 15 years old! We ended up having a massive fight. Bob kept asking what I was going to do to improve my behavior. I responded with "I don't know." I did not even know I had a behavior problem. I don't mean that sarcastically I really did not think I had a problem. The conversation was not getting any better. In fact, it became somewhat violent. I ended up running out the front door and ran to a friend's house. All the way there I kept thinking "I hope he is home."

When I got to Tim's house I knocked at the front door. I was so glad to see Tim's mother. She invited me in and told me Tim was in his bedroom. When I walked in, he was really surprised to see me, and I was happy to see him as well. As I looked around his room I noticed that he had everything packed. When I asked what was going on, he said he was going to stay with his grandparents for a while. I must

Fire and Faith

have had a saddened look on my face, because he asked me "What's the matter?" I told him that I could not stay at my own house, and that I needed a place to go. Tim told me that he would ask his grandmother if I could stay there for a while with him. If she said yes, we would be leaving in the morning. Luckily, his grandmother said yes, and we were on our way to his grandmother's house the following morning. I called my mother and told her over the phone, that I would be moving about seventy miles away. She came by with about fifty dollars so I could give it to Tim's grandmother. I knew in my heart that staying at his grandmother's house was only temporary.

Tim had to start school that following Monday and I stayed at the house. I think it was about a week and I finally decided to get myself into school as well. The days were very boring at the house, and I wanted to get to know some people. I met a girl right off the bat, and I was at her house every day after school. Every day the routine was the same. Her parents were never home so we would always have sex and drink alcohol at her house after school. That's all we ever did. That was the extent of our relationship. This relationship only lasted about month before I was off with another girl.

At Tim's house, we played music in the garage every night. It was a party at all times. There was always alcohol and weed there, so we were always bombed, or stoned every night. Tim would play the drums and I would play guitar. We had dreams of making into "the big time". We actually had a few original songs, and we thought that was all we needed. Our dream was cut short when Tim's grandparents wanted me to move on. I did not do anything wrong, but it was a small house, and I had already been there for a couple of months. I had no idea where I was going to go. I was fifteen years old, and I needed a place to live again. I had to call my mother to tell her that Tim's grandparents were going to be dropping me off in Hesperia. My mother said that I could stay at the house for a bit, but we would need to talk when she got home.

I had Tim's grandmother drop me off at the high school in Hesperia. I figured if I enrolled myself, that would show to my mother and Bob that I was trying to be a better kid. After getting the enrollment done, I walked home. By the time I got there my mother and Bob were already there at the house. When I got to the house my mother met me at the door, and gave me a hug. She was so happy to see me, and as usual Bob blamed me for screwing up at Tim's house. Bob asked me where I had been. I told him that I was at the high school enrolling for class. He asked me why I was going to school. He said ditch diggers did not need an education. He said that I would never amount to anything. My mother quickly interrupted and said "That's enough." She did not want to hear the arguing. Once again, I felt as if I was nothing. In my head at the time no one loved me. I felt like I was the mistake and not that I had made mistakes. Once again, I was starting to feel as if there was nothing to live for. I think the only thing that pulled me out of this slump was the possibility of going to school and meeting girls.

I started school that Monday morning. I knew some of the kids from when I had attended junior high there before. I quickly made a few new friends. As usual, they were always getting high, smoking and drinking. I really tried to make an effort not to start drinking and getting high, but even that effort eventually fell by the way side. I was back in my normal groove of getting loaded. I had been told all my life that I would never amount to anything, so why try now? I found myself getting high constantly and began to fail school. I had only been there for a couple of months. I knew I was not going to pass the tenth grade, so why bother? I had already been to so many schools, and I was so far behind, I simply gave up. The news of failing school made its way to my parents through the mail.

I remember coming home one day from school and it was pretty late. I decided rather than go straight home I would hang out with my friends after school. I did not expect my parents to get home before

Fire and Faith

me. Like I mentioned before, they worked so far away and they usually did not get home until about five o'clock. When I walked in the house they immediately asked where I had been. What hit me was that they really did not care where I was. What they cared about was the fact that I was not home when they got home. They were not worried about me. They only knew that I did not do as I was told. They went on to tell me that I was supposed to come home right after school, and when I got home, I was supposed to get my chores done. They told me that I needed to come and sit with them in the living room while they talked to me. The sad part was that they never talked to me. It was more like, "Let's tell Joey what piece of crap he is, and see if Joey gets mad, and when he does, we will tell him to shut up. Then, if Joey does not shut up, we will ground him. And when Joey tries to speak his feelings, we will kick Joey out and send him away." This type of living condition is what drove me to think that I was useless and no good. In my mind there was no reason to live, but for some reason I did continue on but it was for all the wrong reasons.

I decided that this time, I was not going to stay silent. I was going to finally speak up, whether I was crying (or not), my feelings were going to be heard. I remember this like it was yesterday. The lecture was near the end, and before Bob finished his long winded speech about how I would once again not amount to anything in life, I stood up out of my chair. Bob was pissed that I stood up and yelled "Where do you think you're going?" I told him "I did not have to listen to you put me down anymore." Bob sat in his mighty chair and said "Oh, you don't huh?" I turned to walk away and go down the hallway to get away from him. He kept yelling "Where are you going tough guy?" I was probably twenty feet away from him when he through his glass ashtray at me. I moved my head just in time. The ashtray whizzed by me and got stuck in the wall. I turned around and yelled, "What is your problem!" Bob was getting up out of his chair and yelled, "You are my problem!"

Bob ran through the living room towards me at a full-sprint. Somehow my mother got up just as fast and was right behind him. Bob was already swinging his arms to hit me. I kept ducking and moving backwards all the way into their room. I made to their bathroom and locked the door. I could hear Bob just outside the door calling me out. He was screaming at the top of his lungs calling names. My mother was out there yelling, "Calm down! Bob calm down!" As I stood in the bathroom looking in the mirror at myself watching the tears roll down my face, I decided at that point I had enough. I was going to open the door and go at it with Bob, and I was not going to lose. I had full intention of walking out there and kicking his butt.

When I pull the door open I could hear them arguing in the hallway. I ran out of his bedroom and down the hallway I went. I was within a couple of feet from him and I realized my mother was standing in between us. He looked over her shoulder and said, "What? Do you want to do this? Come on then!" He took a swing at me and missed. I guess seeing my mother in the middle of us, I felt that maybe she would end up getting hurt. I just stood behind and watched him act like an idiot trying to get at me. My mother was not moving though. That's when I realized I needed to get out of the hallway. I figured he was going to end up hitting my mother to get to me. I stepped into my bedroom and slammed the door. I looked around the room to see what I could use to bust his head open. I had full intention to hurt this man. I decided that was the wrong thing to do. My next decision was to leave.

I could not catch my breath. I was breathing so hard, as I looked for things to take with me, all the while hearing Bob yelling at my mother to get out of the way. I decided I only needed a jacket and that was it. I remembered my bedroom window was open, and I ran as fast I could to make the jump through the window. I only took out the screen with

Fire and Faith

my body, but even then I knew Bob would have to replace it and that

would piss him off. I ran as fast I could to Tim's old house where his

mother still lived. Tim's mother was a sweetheart to me. She always

accepted me in when things went bad at my house. My mother knew I

must have gone there, because she called the house about an hour later.

My mother told me that she was going to come by in a few minutes

because she had something to tell me. I hung up the phone, and I

walked out in front of Tim's house where I waited for my mother. She

showed up minutes later with 5 dollars for me so I could get something

to eat. My mother said that enough was enough. I truly thought to

myself "Finally! She woke up and we going to be free from all the

crap." I believed that we would be able to live our lives without abuse.

She told me that she was going to leave Bob, and that we were going to

move to Arizona and stay with my grandparents. She told me

"Everything is going to be ok now. You should call me about eight

o'clock in the morning". Then she was going to pick me up, and we

were leaving.

I woke up the following morning, and quickly called my mother.

When she answered the phone something did not sound right. My

mother told me that we would not be going to Arizona. My mother

went on to say that she and Bob worked things out. I was so let down,

Fire and Faith

and I figured that our lives were never going to change. I asked my mother about what I was supposed to do. She asked me if I could stay at Tim's house for a little while just until Bob cooled down. I asked how long that was going to be before he was calm enough for me to come back home. I truly did not want to go back, but I had no place to go. My mother told that she was not sure, but it would probably take some time. The problem was, I did not have time, and I definitely had no place to go. I was only fifteen. It's not like I could get a job or an apartment. I asked Tim's mother if I could stay for a few days, and she said yes.

Chapter 11

I stayed there one more night at Tim's house, and called another friend
mine to come and pick me up. His name was Larry and he was going
to a party out in the desert. On Friday and Saturday nights all the
teenagers would go to a place called "Blacks Bridge." There would be
kegs of beer, drugs and friends. It was the beginning of fall and desert
got very cold at night. The only clothes I had were the ones that I was
wearing. Before Larry got there on Friday, I decided to go to my house
and grab some clothes and a jacket. The doors were locked, so I had to
get in through one of the windows at my house.

Once I got inside I remembered Bob had a change jar in the
bedroom, so I helped myself to about 10 dollars. As I was grabbing the
change, I thought about Bob's pistol by the bed. This time I tried
something a little more dangerous. I remembered a movie that came a
long time where the men played Russian roulette. This is where one
bullet is left in the gun and the chamber is spun and stopped quickly.
Then the trigger is pulled and if the gun does not fire then you live. If
it does fire, well you get the point. I tried it one time, and obviously the
gun did not fire. I wasted no time, I just pulled the trigger! I remember
my body to the core was shaking on the inside after I pulled the trigger.

Fire and Faith

I instantly started sweating and my heart raced. I put the bullets back into the pistol and put the gun back. I never again put a pistol to my head, at least by my own doing.

After getting the change, I also went out to the kitchen, and took a couple packs of cigarettes out of each carton, that was on top of the refrigerator. I grabbed some food and something to drink while I was there as well. I took a quick shower and got dressed. I grabbed a duffle bag and filled it with clothes and whatever else I thought I might need. Larry came and picked me up at my parents' house, and we were on our way to go party the night away. I had no idea at this point what the future for me looked like. I had no plans, no idea where I might be staying, or even going for that night.

We got to the bridge and there were at least three-hundred people there partying. There were huge bon-fires, loud music, and laughter. There were cars parked everywhere. It was like Disneyland for partiers. I remember getting out of Larry's car and we blended in the mix fast. I drank one beer after another. The smell of people smoking weed was heavy in in the air. There was a girl there that I thought was pretty cute, so I went over to her. We talked for a little while, when she asked me if I wanted to get high. I said to her sure so I reached in my pocket and pulled out a joint. I figured we would smoke a little weed and move directly into sex. She said she did not smoke weed, and that she had something different. She pulled out a tiny plastic bag, with what looked like a bunch of little white rocks in it. I actually thought she had a bag of salt rocks. I asked her what it was, and she said "Crystal meth." I told her that I had never done that before, but I was willing to do it with her. She dumped part of the bag out onto a pocket sized mirror. I asked her if this was coke and she told me no. She told me this was way better than coke.

After grinding all the rocks up into a fine powder, she sniffed a small pile of it. Then she handed me the mirror with the remaining pile and said "Here you go." I remember sniffing the whole pile, and my nose felt like it was on fire. Within about 15 minutes I was high. Everything seemed to be extremely focused. I could breathe like I have breathed before. It was so euphoric. The feeling was amazing to me and better than any other high that I had experienced. My sex drive seemed to be in overdrive. I told her that I was really horny, and she said "Good. The meth is working." Shortly after, we had sex, and it was amazing. I had never been able to last for so long. It took about an hour before I was able to climax. After we had finished we talked for hours. It was almost as if I could not stop talking. I kept drinking beers and I was not getting drunk. The drugs kept me from getting drunk. To me at the time was amazing. The drug kept me wide awake and talking for hours.

During our talk, she asked me where I lived and I told her that I did not have a place to live. She told me that if I rode home with her that night, she would be able to put me in her parent's camp-trailer that was parked on their property. Most of the houses in Apple Valley and Hesperia at the time also had large property. I was not able to have a light out there, because her parents would know I was out there. At the time, the cool thing for me was that she would sneak out of her house, and stay the night with me. Every time she would bring more crystal meth with her. Then she would go back in her house just before sun-up. When a person uses crystal meth, they often cannot sleep or eat for a few days, depending on how much a person uses. Eventually the person's body just shuts down, and they fall asleep.

I think I was there for about a week and half, when I ended up with the flu. During this time, my biggest problem besides the flu was finding food. I could not just walk to the fridge and grab something to eat. The only thing I had was mayonnaise sandwiches. My girlfriend could not take too much more than that from the house, because she was afraid of being caught. My flu started to get worse, and my coughing was out of control. I would cough so hard that my girlfriend

Fire and Faith

told me that she could hear me all the way from the house. If I was
caught in the trailer, it would have caused a serious problem. I am sure
that her parents would have either called the cops and had me arrested,
(which probably would have been the best thing for me), or she would
have been in big trouble for hiding me. Another big concern for me
was bathing. I could only get into her house when both of her parents
were not home. That seems like it would be easy, but her mother was a
stay-at-home mom. When her mother went shopping, which was once
a week, that's when I was able to get in and shower.

I decided it would be best that I left. I figured if I made it back to
bridge, I would find someone that I knew, and I could go to their place
for a couple of nights or so. The bridge was really far from where I
was though, so I needed a place stay along the way. Needing to find a
warm place to stay, I found an empty house. I was really sick, weak
and hungry. All I could think of was that I had to get out of the cold
and get something to eat. About a half-mile from the empty house, I
found a corner store. First, I went to the house to make sure I would be
able to leave my stuff there. The houses there were each on an acre of
land. This made it very easy for me to get in undetected by any
neighbors. Once inside I set my stuff down and checked to see if there

Fire and Faith

was power in the house. Thank God for me there was. I never turned the lights on though; I only turned the heat on to keep warm.

After I put my stuff in one of the empty closets, I made my way down to the corner store. I had no money for anything so when I walked in; I made sure that there was no one inside except me and the cashier. I went to the back of the store and grabbed a half gallon of milk, and made my way up the isle and grabbed a bottle of cough syrup. Just to the left of the medicine isle was where the hamburgers and hot dogs were cooking on the warmers. As I filled the courtesy bags with three hamburgers and two hot dogs, I could feel the sweat running down my forehead from my fever. I walked straight up to counter and reached my hand above the register and grabbed a pack of cigarettes. The man behind the counter asked "What the hell are you doing?" I did not even look at him. Without hesitation, I ran for the door. I ran so fast that when I pushed the door open, I cracked the glass. I remember hearing the cashier yelling from the counter. He was screaming "Get back here you punk!" I thought for sure he was going to chase me, and if he did I was prepared to fight for what I just taken. As I rounded the corner on the backside of the store, I looked over my shoulder and he was not there. I ran the long way to the house I was "squatting" in.

Fire and Faith

When I got back to the house it was getting close to dark. I got in the house quickly and sat down to catch my breath. I could not stop coughing, and the sweat was so bad that my shirt was soaked. I started thinking that if I had heat, then I must have hot water. I took all my clothes off and got in the shower. When I think about it now, I have never had a better shower than that night. The water was so hot and felt so good. I remember looking down at my feet as the water ran down body and turned the bottom of the tub black. I must not have been thinking too clearly though. I had no towel. I had to use a shirt that I had in my duffle bag to dry off. Once I dried off, I made my way to the living room. I used the remaining clothes I had to make a bed. I took a few sips of the cough medicine to try and quiet down my cough, but even that did not work. Later I found out, the Russian flu was going around and that is what I'd had.

I planned on staying at this house for at least a couple of days, until I was feeling better. The problem was I was not getting any better. I just could not stop coughing, but at least I was warm. When I woke up the following morning, I ate some of the food I had stolen the night before. I was so hungry, but I could not eat a lot. My stomach would not allow me to eat large quantities of food. I could only take about 3 bites, before I felt like I was going to get sick. I put the food aside and tried to get some more sleep. I started thinking that I would like to get more meth and just the thought of the drug kept me awake. Finally by the time it got dark outside I fell asleep. I remember waking up a lot throughout the night. I would have twenty- minute coughing fits and then I finally fall back to sleep. If I had to guess now, I finally fell into a deep sleep around three or four o'clock in the morning.

When I woke up, there was a man, his wife and kids coming through the front door. I don't know who was more freaked out: Me being in the house, or them finding me in their house. When I looked at him, I expected him to yell at me to get out of his house, but he didn't. In fact I was so rushed grabbing my stuff to get out, the man never even said a thing. I kept saying over and over again that I was sorry, and that I just needed a warm place to stay. I kept looking out of the corner of my eye to watch them while I packed all of my stuff. I remember his wife looked at him with sadness in her eyes. She kept looking to her husband for him to say something. She was not mad. I saw more compassion from her.

As I grabbed the last bit of my stuff, I made my way to the front door. I said sorry one last time to them, as I walked out and shut the front door. I made my way back to the bridge where everybody partied on the weekends. I hid my stuff in some bushes close to the bridge. I could hear people talking below the bridge. When I made my way down the side of the hill, I ran into a couple of guys sitting there at the bottom getting high. One of the guys looked really familiar to me. I must have looked familiar to him, because he thought he knew me as well. We started talking trying to figure out how we knew each other. He told me his name was Jimmy, and I told him my name is Joey. We could not come up with an answer, but he did invite me to sit down and have a beer and get high. Before I knew it he asked me if I wanted to hang out with him for a while that day. I had no problem doing that. He took me back to where he lived and we stayed there for the awhile.

He had no electricity in the house he was living in, but it did not matter to me. He did have a lot weed though, and we got high enough that the cold was not so bothersome. He had so a lot of weed. I wondered where he got it from. So, when I asked him, he said "Can you keep a secret?" I told him that would not be a problem. He walked to backside of the house and through a red door. When he opened the door, I saw close to two-hundred marijuana plants. They were huge! Each plant was about five feet tall. He told me that he was getting ready to sell them all and then start all over again with a new crop. On the other side of the room there were about two-hundred smaller plants that need to be transplanted to bigger pots. He told me told me that if I helped him, he would give me a portion of the money. He told there were risks involved, like getting caught by the law. I did not care though. I was all in. We went back into the living room, and I remember it was starting to get dark. We sat for about another hour or so, when he said he was going to bed. I remember lying there thinking about what I would do with my share of the money. The first thing I was going to do was get food.

I woke that morning to the guy slugging me in the head and chest. He was screaming at me calling me every name in the book. He wanted to know where all the plants were. It took me a few seconds to realize that he must have been robbed and thought I did it. I fought him the best that I could. He was winning this fight, and at one point I got a good shot in and he fell back to the floor. I kept telling him that I did not do anything, but he was not listening. Finally, I told him that there was no way that I could take that many plants and hide them. "Really" I said, "How could I hide that many plants being on foot?" It took some convincing, but he finally started to listen. He said that we were going to go to the bridge that night to see if anyone at the party had a lot of weed to sell or use.

When we got to the bridge that night, I saw the girl I had stayed with just the week prior. I went to her right off the bat. I was looking for

Fire and Faith

sex and meth and she was ready for both. She told me that she needed

to buy more meth. She asked if I had any money and I told her that I

didn't. She said it wouldn't be a problem, and that there was a guy that

owed her some money. But, we needed to go and collect it. She said

that he was at a party somewhere, and that we would need to find him.

We finally found him sitting in his car with two other people. She

knocked at his window and he motioned her to get in the car. We both

got into the backseat. He told her that he had her money, and that he

would give it to her in a little bit. Just as he said that someone else

came to his window to buy some weed. He said, "How much you

want?", as leaned over to his glove compartment. When he opened it

there was about a pound of marijuana individually wrapped in bags. At

that moment I instantly thought this was the guy who took my friends

plants.

I did not say a word about it to him. One thing I learned when I was

on the streets was that no one could keep their mouth shut. When it

came to stealing, it seemed thieves always wanted to brag about it.

Within ten minutes, he began to tell how he had stolen all of the

marijuana plants. I still did not say a word about it. My only concern

was that she got her drugs and then we would be alone together. We

ended up staying in this guy's car for the rest of the night. The sun was coming up, and he said that everybody should meet again the next weekend. I told him that I would be there the next weekend. The girl that I wanted to be with went with him, and he took her home. I looked for the guy that I came with that night and I could not find him. He must have gone home. Now, not only did I not have food, but I also had no place to stay.

The bridge we were at was about four miles from town, and I decided to leave my stuff hidden in the bushes and go into town. I thought to myself that I really needed to get something to eat. Along the way, I came to a convenience store and decided I was going to steal what I needed to eat. I walked in the store, and I felt my heart racing. I was not as confidant as I was the first time I'd done this. I walk to the back of the store and grabbed a thing of bologna and a loaf of bread. Then, I walked to the front of the store, and turned quickly to the left and ran. I ran as fast as I could, and looked for a place to hide. There was an underpass just about a block away. I quickly ran down the side of the bridge and hid there. When I started looking around, I saw old clothing and empty liquor bottles everywhere. I figured that I would stay there for the night because it seemed pretty warm. The bridge above had heavy traffic, and it was warm beneath because of all the cars above. As it started to get dark, people or "bums" started to come down to bed down for the night. No one looked at me or even talked to me. I put some distance between me and the bums. I remember I started getting pretty tired and I fell asleep. When I woke up, the food that I had stolen was gone. Even worse, someone had stolen my shoes right off my feet while I was sleeping!

Now I needed to get shoes, and I still had no money. There was a mall about a mile and half up the road. I walked to the mall, and entered through JC Penny's. I immediately went to the shoe department and wasted no time finding the shoes that I wanted. I tried them on, and they fit perfect. As I walked over to the clothing side, the exit door was within a few feet from me. I hesitated and when I finally got the courage to run, a man grabbed my shoulder. He said "Where are you going?" He turned me around and started to walk me in the opposite direction. He told me that he already called the police and that they were on their way. We walked a few more feet, and I turned quickly to break his hold on me and ran for the door. He was right behind me as I went through the door to the parking lot. I kept telling myself that he was not going to catch me no matter what. I kept running as fast as I could and when I turned to look he was nowhere in sight. I could not believe that he gave up, so I kept running. I finally came to the realization that he was not there anymore, and I slowed

Fire and Faith

down. As I walked down the sidewalk trying to catch my breath, I looked to right of me and saw an unemployment office. I was only fifteen years old, but I figured they would be able to help me find a job. I did not want have to steal anymore, and I really wanted money to be able to buy food.

I walked across the parking lot, and went through the door. I really did not even know what I was supposed to do once I got in there. I went to the front counter, and a lady asked how she could help me. I told her that I needed to find a job. She gave me a ticket with a number on it, and told me to have a seat. I remember looking around the big office and seeing a lot of people. There were many women there with babies. All of the babies were crying and the office smelled horrible. I waited for close to half an hour, and then I heard my number called. I stood up and walked in between a row of cubicles before I got to the one I needed to be at. There in the cubicle was an older beautiful women seated at her desk. She looked up, and asked me "What can I help you with?" I told her that I needed a job. She tilted her head slightly and told me to have a seat. She asked me what kind of work experience I had. I told her that I knew how to build a house. With a smile she said "Oh, you can huh?" I told her that my grandfather had taught me at a very young age. She said "Speaking of age, how old are

Fire and Faith

you?" I am fifteen, and that I was turning 16 in February. She said that she could not help me, and that I would need a parent's signature to allow me to work.

At that very moment I started to cry. Everything seemed so overwhelming to me at that point. I was so hungry and so afraid of what was going to happen to me. She asked me if I was ok. I told that I was going to be fine, but I really needed a job. She pulled her chair around the desk and placed it in front of me. She sat down and asked "What is going on?" I told her that I was living on the streets, and I really needed to work so I could by food. I did not care where I lived, I was just so hungry. She stood up and looked around the office. She then crouched down and reached for her purse. She told me that she was not allowed to this, and for me not to say a word. She reached in her wallet and pulled out five dollars and handed it to me. She told me that the best thing I could do was to go home. I was really underweight and looked horrible. She told me that she was not trying to be mean, but that she was concerned for me. I started to feel like I was going to breakdown and cry again, so I stood up and thanked her for her time. I made my way back to the door and left.

The first thing I did was head to the grocery store. I bought a quart of chocolate milk and a box of Little Debbie Oatmeal snack cakes. I

Fire and Faith

walked outside and headed to the back of the store. I sat down and

leaned against the wall. The sun was shining on my face and it was

very warm. I started getting very sleepy but I kept trying to wake

myself up. I did not want to fall asleep and have my food stolen. I

think I ate about five of the cakes and drank all the chocolate milk. I

was feeling pretty energized, and I decided to walk back to the

underpass wear I slept the night before. When I got there, I saw an old

man that going through his own stuff. I started looking to see if he had

my shoes. He saw me looking at him and he asked what I was looking

at. I told him that I been there last night, and while I was sleeping

someone had stolen my shoes. The old man smiled at me and said

"You have a lot to learn if you are going to make it here." I said to him

"I like the fact that there are other people here, and I am not alone.

What I don't like is that I have to sleep with one eye open." The old

man laughed again and said "Take your shoes off and tie them around

your wrists. That way you'll wake up if anyone else tries to steal

them."

Darkness was starting to fall on the day, and the bums came under

the bridge one by one. I remember doing a head count, and there was

seventeen people including myself under that bridge. I made sure that I

put enough distance between myself and the bums. I also took my new

Fire and Faith

shoes off and tied them around my wrists, just like the old man told me to. I did not sleep to well that night, but I knew that I was not going to be robbed for my shoes. It was pretty cold that night and when I woke that morning there was a blanket on me. When I rolled over, everyone was already gone. I remember thinking to myself that I needed to get cleaned up. I had not bathed in a while and I was starting to smell. I actually thought of going to the fishery that was done street to bathe. The water was temperature controlled and it would be better than getting in the cold water of the stream.

I packed up my stuff, and buried it just on the other side of the bridge. I buried my duffle bag in leaves and sticks so no one could see it. I made my way down to the fishery and took my clothes off down to my underwear and got in. The water was still cold, but not near as cold as the stream. I wasted no time getting as clean as possible and getting out. I quickly dried off and got dressed. I headed out to a store to try and get something to eat. I still had a little over 2 dollars left from the 5 dollars; the lady at the unemployment office gave me. I went into the store and stole a bar of soap and bought more food for the day. I spent several days and nights at the bridge and waited for the weekend. I knew that everyone would be back to party at the other bridge and I was not going to miss out. I just wanted to get high.

Fire and Faith

The weekend finally came, and I made my way down to the party spot. I got there really early, and I saw the guy that had stolen all the marijuana plants just sitting in his car. When he saw me, he flagged me down to come over to the car. I quickly made my way over to him, and got in the car. He was alone and getting high. We reintroduced ourselves, and he told me his name was Rob. Rob asked me where I lived and when I told him my situation he said I was welcome to stay with him for a while. Rob was not much better off. He was living in his car. Rob had a yellow 70's model Nova, and it was pretty beat up. I figured it would be warmer than staying under the bridge. The upside to this was that I only had to worry about one person, rather than a group of people robbing me or beating me up.

He explained to me that we had to go pick up the girl that I had been seeing. I asked how long he had known her, and he said for about few months. He told me that she really liked me and that she wanted to see me tonight at the part, so we left and went to get her. When she got in the car she reached in her pocket and pulled out that small bag loaded with meth. I knew this was going to be a great night. We started doing line after line of it. After sniffing each line, my nose felt like it was on fire. My hunger pains quickly went away, and I was ready to party. We headed back to the bridge and started the night. When you get high on meth, it is really difficult to get drunk. You can drink as much beer as you want and not get drunk. We stayed with the crowd for about an hour before my girlfriend and I headed back to the car to be alone.

After we were finished fooling around we made our way back to the party. I could hear people yelling and arguing. Through the crowd, I could hear Jimmy accusing Rob for stealing all of his marijuana plants. He was shoving Rob, and Jimmy's friend soon joined in. When Jimmy saw me walk up, he thought I had to be involved because I was hanging out with Rob. I remember telling him that I had nothing to do with it. He would not listen to me and quickly began fighting. There were other people trying to split us up, and as quickly as it started, we were getting in to the car and leaving. Rob was so mad, and he kept saying "What am I going to do for money now?" My girlfriend spoke up and said that she knew of a house that could be robbed. She went on to say that the people only lived there in the summer. She said there were all kinds of things in the house that we could sell to make money. Rob agreed and said that we should go that night.

I remember the house seemed like it was out in the middle nowhere. It was a large house and sat on the side of a hill. In a way, it almost seeming haunting to me. There were other houses around it, but it was so late at night everyone was probably asleep. We drove down the dirt

Fire and Faith

road that led to the house. Each house sat on at least an acre. There were no lights on in any of the homes we drove by. I asked my girlfriend if they were all empty and she said no. She went on to say that this was the only house that was empty during the winter months. We drove down the road with the lights off so we would not attract attention. When we pulled into the driveway I kept asking her if she was sure they were not home. She kept saying to me "Stop be paranoid." Rob shut the car off and got out. We followed him while he walked around the yard. He came across a small trailer and he decided to hitch it to his car. He figured we could fit more stuff in that way. I was so scared. I kept feeling that someone was in the house watching us.

After Rob finished hitching the trailer, he said "Let's get this on." We walked around to the front of the house, and made our way up the stairs. We walked very cautiously so we would not make noise. When we reached the top of the stairs, Rob reached for the door knob. When he turned the knob, he found that it was locked. I reached out to the living room window and slid it open. It was as if they wanted to be robbed. I climbed in through the window and made my way to the front door. I still had an eerie feeling that someone was inside. I walked quietly through the house checking each room. To my surprise

Fire and Faith

there was no one there. We started looking through all the dresser drawers in the bedrooms. I was looking for small items that would get a lot of money, but when I walked out to the living room, Rob was taking furniture. I said "What the hell are you doing?" There was no way that we had time for all this stuff to be loaded. We were arguing in the living room when out of the corner my eye, I saw a light turn on in the distance at a neighbor's house. I told him we needed to get out of there before someone called the cops. My girlfriend said, "Relax. The neighbor was probably getting up to go to the bathroom." Rob continued to load all the big appliances and furniture. By the time we were done, the trailer was completely full.

We got into the car and started down the road. The neighboring house still had the light on. As we passed the house, I saw a man standing in the driveway with a gun. As we passed by him he pointed right at me in the car. The man pulled the trigger and fired a shot at me. He missed me by inches and hit the inside of the driver's door. I yelled at Rob and told him to "Go! Go!" Rob stepped on the gas and took off. I watched the man who'd just shot at me head for his car. As we passed the third house a man in a Jeep pulled out of his driveway. He was now part of the chase. Rob still had his headlights off and it was pitch-black outside. The only lights that I saw were the ones that were behind us, and they were getting closer.

They chased us for a few minutes, and were right behind us. There was no way we were going to lose them with the trailer hitched to the car, not to mention it was weighed down with all the furniture in it. We were still a long way from any town or any heavy populated area. All the homes out there were as big as farms. I started to think that we were going to get caught sooner or later. I remember looking down at my feet, and saw a bunch of beer bottles. Some were empty and some were still unopened. I reached down and grabbed an unopened bottle, pulled myself up into the open window, and threw the bottle at the vehicle behind us. I hit his windshield, and he lost control of the vehicle. He was now out of the chase, but there was still the guy that shot at me. I reached for another bottle threw that as well. I hit his vehicle and watched to see if he was going to give up. Then I saw his arm come outside of his window and fired another shot at me. He missed me again, and I said to Rob, "Just get off the road! Go through the fields!" Rob swung the car and trailer off the road into someone's farm. As Rob drove through this farm I watched the headlights of the pursuing vehicle get further and further away. I was really happy we lost him driving through the farm. When we got to the other side of the farm, we ended up on a dirt road. I said to Rob, "Drop the trailer and just drive away." He argued with me and said, "I'm not going to lose everything especially after everything we just went through."

Rob kept the trailer, and I kept looking to see if anyone was following us. I asked him where he was going with all of the stuff. He said "I'm taking it to your girlfriend's house, and trade it for drugs." When he said that turned to look at my girlfriend and said to her "What does he mean by that?" I did not know it, but her mother was a big time drug dealer. That's how my girlfriend always had crystal meth. We were on the road for at least thirty minutes. Rob kept driving in circles to make sure he was not being followed. When we finally made it to her house, the sun was just starting to come up. We pulled into the driveway, and started to unload the trailer into her backyard. My girlfriend's mother came outside to see what was going on. My girlfriend told her the whole story and how we were shot at. Her mother thought that story was humorous, and told us to come in and relax for a bit.

I remember walking in the house and there were all kinds of paraphernalia lying on the kitchen table. She offered us some meth to snort, and I was planned on taking the biggest amount possible. I looked around for a cigarette just after I got high. I was still shaking

Fire and Faith

from what had happened. Rob and my girlfriend talked about me like I was some kind of hero for throwing the beer bottles. I did not think of myself that way though. I was still really scared. I also kept thinking we were going to be caught. We stayed at her house the next couple of days to lay low. I did so much meth that I did not sleep. I was starting to hallucinate, from the lack of sleep and food. We would stay up at night until her mother went to bed, and then I would go in her room so we could be alone. While we were having sex, I kept hallucinating that there were people in the room sitting next to us by a waterfall. I kept telling her that there were people in the room with us. She kept telling me that there weren't, but I insisted. She got so upset with me that she told me to get out of her room. She told me that I had to leave when Rob did. I walked out to the living room and tried to sleep. I finally fell asleep just before sunrise and I slept until 3 that afternoon.

I woke to Rob saying "We have to go." My girlfriend's dad was going to be home soon, and we could not be caught there. I was so tired. I could not keep my eyes open. Just before we left I asked how we were getting paid for all the stolen stuff. Rob said "I already got the money, but we have to leave right now." I got up off the couch and looked at my girlfriend, but she wanted nothing to do with me. I couldn't figure out why she was so mad at me and I never did. We walked out of the house and got into the car. I asked Rob where we were going and he said that he knew of an abandoned house that we were going to go stay at. I did not care where we went as long as I could sleep.

I had been up for almost four days and I only had about seven hours of sleep. We pulled up to the house that Rob had been talking about. This house did not even have roof. It was basically only four walls. It was obvious that house had been on fire at some point. When we got out of the car it was really windy and cold. We went into the backside of the house that had a partial roof on it still. The house had a fireplace that was still standing. We made a fire and sat on the remaining burned out furniture. I was so hungry, and Rob had a few cans of stew and soup. We placed them into the fire to heat up. Nothing is worse than having hot food you cannot eat. We had no can opener, so we ended up using a pocket knife to stab the can over and over again. Finally, after making enough holes in the lids, we were able to tip the food out of the cans and into our mouths.

We went to sleep that night with full bellies. When I woke up that next morning, I felt pretty good. I got about ten hours of much needed rest. The first thing I wanted to do was get my hands on some meth. I wanted to get high, and remembered Rob said he gotten money for the stuff we had stolen just a few days back. I asked Rob when we were going to go get more speed or "meth." He said that he did not have any money at all. I asked him what he was talking about. He told me that she paid him with speed and food. So I asked him where the speed was. I just wanted to get high, I really did not care if we got money or not. He had enough speed for the both us and probably ten more people to get high. We sat down on the half burnt couch and divided up the speed. I did half of mine right then without hesitation. I knew that if I was high the world would not seem so bad to me. We packed up what we had and headed back to the party bridge.

When we got to the bridge we spent the next few days there high, and waited for Friday night to come around. On occasion, we would drive to different stores and do "beer runs". I would walk in and grab two twelve-packs and run out of the store. I grabbed two because I thought if the cashier chased me, I would be able to throw one twelve pack at him to slow him down. When Friday night finally came around we knew that it would be party time. We were going to trade off all the beer that we had been saving up for speed. It was probably around nine o'clock at night, but there were only a handful of people. Normally, there would have been a couple of hundred. I guess it was getting too cold to be out there partying. Rob and I decided to stay there until

Fire and Faith

Saturday night and see if more people showed up, but there was no change. In fact there were less people this time. Rob said that we would leave in the morning to go to his aunt's house to stay there for a while. I was pretty tired considering I had been up for another 4 days. I ended up falling asleep on the ground by the fire, and when I woke, I was alone. Rob had packed his crap up and left. At first, I thought he must have gone to the store, but after a couple of hours he still had not returned. That was the last time I ever saw Rob again.

I ended up making my way back to the second bridge where all the bums stayed at. In some strange way it felt like home. I don't really mean home, but it was very familiar with the same people. Once again though, when night fell, I was cold and hungry. A new problem was starting to bother me now. My back and the top of my left arm were really itchy. It was the kind of itch that made you want to use a garden rake to scratch it. When I pulled my shirt back and looked at my shoulder I noticed a ring about the size of quarter on my skin. I did not know it then, but I had ringworm on my arms and back. I continued to stay under the bridge for a long time. Days turned to weeks and week into months. I would occasionally steal food to eat. I could not do it all the time because I was running out of stores. All the cashiers knew who I was, and I did not want to press my luck. I started getting really weak and knew I needed to go home. I had been gone for a long time.

I know I was gone for more than six months. I lived on the streets with

bums, and drug addicts at the age of fifteen and I survived…Tell me I

did not have someone above looking out for me. I just did not know it

yet.

I was not doing well, and like I mentioned before, it was time for me

to get home. I figured I would rather live with Bob and his somewhat

cruel ways, than live under the bridge. I walked into town to beg for

change so I could call my mother. When I called, a message played

that said "This number is no longer in service." I was a long way from

home; at least twenty miles away. There was no way I would make it

walking. I called the neighbor next door to my parents' house, and

asked them to give me my parents new phone number. I remember she

said "Oh dear. They move away a long time ago." She asked me if

everything was ok, and I said "Thank you anyway. I'll try someone

else." I had no more change, so I went back to bridge for the night. I

was broken hearted that my own mother could leave me behind.

"When I look at my children now I think to myself that there would be

no way I could leave them like that. I could not move away and be

okay with that."

Chapter 12

I stayed at the bridge that night, and I could not sleep. The only thing I could think of is how could my mother move without me. I kept imagining her driving away in the moving truck looking out the window wondering where I was. Then I thought, 'Did she even care that I was out there somewhere?' I kept thinking, I am her only child, and it bugged me to no end that she could leave me like that. I finally fell asleep and woke up the next morning with a bad stomach ache.

I made my way back to town and begged for more change. I got enough change to place a call to where my mother worked. It was long distance and I had 3 minutes to describe where I was at. I was not even sure if she worked there, or if she would even want to come and get me. When I called she answered the phone. I told her "You have to come and get me, or I am going to die out here." She was crying as soon as she heard my voice. She asked me where I was at, and I described it as best as I could. She told me to give her the number of the pay phone I was at so she could call me when she got closer. She worked down the mountain, and it was going to be about an hour and half before she could get to me. She told said to me, "Please don't leave, and stay right there by the phone."

Fire and Faith

I sat myself down on an old tire with all my stuff and waited. To me it seemed like hours, but in fact it was about an hour when she finally called me back. She was only about ten minutes up the road. When I saw the car coming down the road I felt relieved. I started to cry and when I looked in the window of the car, my mother was crying too. She jumped out of the car and took my stuff and placed it in the back seat. She pushed the seat back and said "Get in." I told her that I was hungry, and that I needed something to eat. We pulled into a burger joint and I ordered big. I ordered the biggest fries, burger and coke. But I found I could barely eat anything. I asked her what Bob was going to say about me being there at the house, and she told me it did not matter what he thought. I had heard that before, and I did not put too much stock in her words. I asked her one more question, "Where did you move to?" She replied "Ontario, which is about forty-five miles away." For the rest of the trip I did not say another word. I was really tired, and I just wanted to sleep.

When we finally made it back to their new house it was about noon. Believe it or not, I was still chilled to the bone from being under the bridge. I decided that it would be best if I got in the shower. It felt wonderful to let the hot water run down my back. I had not had a shower in weeks. When I got out of the shower, my clothes were gone.

Fire and Faith

My mother had thrown my clothes away. She had some of my older clothes from when I used to live with them for me to wear. When I walked into the bedroom my mother saw my back, and noticed the ringworm. I had large areas of ringworm on my back, and a couple of smaller ones on my shoulder. She told me that we needed to go to the doctor right then to get it taken care of. We got in the car and headed to doctors office. They gave me antibiotic cream. The Doctor said "It's not a big deal. You must have picked it up trying on clothes at the store." He explained that ringworm comes when people don't keep themselves clean and that it was very contagious. He also said it should be cleared up in a couple of weeks.

When we got home from the doctor's office, Bob was already home. My mother walked in first and I followed behind. He did not say a word to me, and that was just fine with me. I just wanted to go to sleep and not worry about being robbed or raped. I went into the room that was prepared for me and I sat down on the bed. I figured I would go straight to sleep, but I didn't. No matter how much I told myself that I was safe, I still did not feel it. It was so quiet in the room I could not stand it. I was used to traffic driving overhead and the occasional argument between the bums. In fact, I was awake most of the night, and did not fall asleep until early morning. When I woke up, my

Fire and Faith

mother and Bob had already gone to work. I got something to eat first thing. I had bacon, eggs and toast. I ate like a king.

I thought I would walk to my mothers work and surprise her, and maybe have lunch with her. I walked in the main office where she had her desk. When I walked in I saw my mother's close friend at her desk. She also worked there as well. When I said hi to her friend, she said "Oh thank God you're here." and then she hung up the phone. I asked "What are you talking about?" I was thinking they thought I ran away again when I didn't answer the phone. I told her that it took me about an hour to walk from the house to the office. She said "No, that's not it. Your mother is in the other office and she is crying." I asked her "What is the problem?" as I walked to the other room where my mother was. She said "You better ask your mother that question."

When I saw my mother she was a crying mess. I went to her and asked her "What's the matter?" She had a hard time talking because she was crying so hard. She finally got the words out saying "I am sorry." I asked "Why are you sorry?" She said "You cannot stay at the house anymore. Bob said you have to leave." I said "I have only been home for one day, and I have not even talked to Bob. There was no way that I could have blown it already. I did not do anything wrong." "I know that. But it's what Bob wants." she said. I paused for a moment and said "It's ok. Where am I going to go?" She said, "I found a homeless shelter down town, and you will be staying there. I asked "When will I be leaving?" "Right now" she replied.

We walked out of the office and made our way to the parking lot. We got in the car and she asked me if I was hungry. I told her that I did want to eat before going to the shelter. I told her that I wanted to get myself enrolled in a program close to the shelter, so I could get my G.E.D. (General Education Diploma). The first place we went to was the house. I needed to pack what little bit I had, so I could have clothes. Then we went to a place called Adult Chaffey College. This is where I would be able to get my G.E.D. When we walked in, my mother had to sign a form for me to be able to study and take the test. I was sixteen now, but they still needed a parent's release. After we were done there we headed off the homeless shelter.

When we arrived there, all I saw was a bunch of bums sitting on the curb. We pulled right in front of the building and we got out of the car. I got my stuff out of the trunk and we headed for the front door of the shelter. We walked up a long staircase and turned the corner into a room that had about thirty beds in it. There was a man there to greet us. He was the gentleman that ran the place. He asked how he could help us. My mother told him that I was going to have to stay there for a

Fire and Faith

while. He had a puzzled look on his face, considering I was so young and obviously her son. He looked at me and started telling me the rules about how things worked there. He told me that I needed to be in early at night so I would be able to get a bed. It was first come, first serve. He put my stuff in a foot locker and told me that everything would stay safe as long as I kept it locked. He asked me if I had any questions for him. I said no. My mother gave me a hug and a kiss and said she "I love you." She kept staring at me as she walked away.

After my mother was out of sight, I opened the locker. I got out a pack of cigarettes that I'd taken from the house. I asked the man where I was allowed to smoke at. He told me if I went back down stairs and to the backside of building, there was an ally. He told me that most of the people that stayed there would be out back as well. When I got down there, I saw a handful of guys smoking and drinking. There was a wall that was about chest high that I went to lean against. I put a smoke in my mouth and lit it. I took a few drags and looked around and when I did I saw a kitten on the wall right next to me. I went right to kitten and picked him up. The kitten was a mess and had been eating out of the dumpster. That kitten crawled up my arm to my shoulder and started purring. This kitten had just become my new best friend. I was out there for about an hour when I heard a man yelling from the upper window of the building. The man was yelling for me to come up there. I took a few more drags off the cigarette, and put the kitten down on the wall. As I made my way around the front of the building, my mother was standing there. I asked her what she wanted and she said that I was going home. I reminded her about what Bob said and she replied that she did not care. As we were getting ready to leave I told her to hang on minute. I ran upstairs and told the man that was running the place to take care of the kitten in the ally. He smiled, and said that he would. I am sure that he didn't, but he made me believe he was going to at the time.

When we got back to the house I unpacked my stuff and got ready for Bob to come home. I figured that this was going to be a war, and I was ready. I figured if he started to raise his voice at me or was condescending in any way, I was going to knock him out. I was not going to take any of his crap that day or any other day. When he did get home, the first thing out of his mouth was, "What is he doing here?" I did not even had chance to say a word, when my mother told me to go outside and give them a little while to talk. I went outside to the garage and had a cigarette. I decided it would be good to take a walk around the neighborhood. I was gone for about an hour or so, before I went back to the house. They were done with their talk when I

Fire and Faith

got back home. When I walked in, my mother said that we were going to eat in just minute, and for me to go wash up. When I came out, I sat at the table and we ate. It was the longest fifteen minutes of my life. The only sound at the table was the silverware sliding across the plates and the swallowing sound of their drinks.

We finished dinner, and I helped my mother carry the dishes to the kitchen, while Bob went back to his chair and watched television. I helped her wash the dishes and not a word was spoken. I decided to go straight to bed after the dishes. I think it was about 6:30 p.m. when I laid down. I was so tired from the events that had taken place that day. I slept straight through the night and woke up early the next morning. I got into the shower and got ready for my first day at the adult school. It was a long walk there, so I got a ride from my mother on her way to work. The purpose of this class was to prepare me for the test. The classes were short, and I was out by 11:00 a.m. Right down the street from the school was a clothing store. I went in after class and applied for job. Surprisingly, I got the job and I started the following day after class.

The job was real easy; all I had to do was fold clothes and put them on the shelf. I worked there the whole time while I was studying for my test. I did not socialize too much while I worked there. I just

Fire and Faith

wanted to do my job and go home. About three months later I was

ready to take the test. I had to miss a day of work to take the exam,

because the only time I could take it was in the afternoon. I remember

walking in the test room, and I was very nervous. I was never a good

test taker. (I still have a hard time to this day.) There were probably

twenty people in the room taking the test as well. The instructor passed

out the first part of the test and told us to start. The first test seemed

very difficult, but I was able to answer to all the questions. I just was

not sure they were the right answers. When we finished the test the

instructor graded them right there on the spot. While the instructor was

grading them I overheard a couple of guys saying that they were going

into the military. The instructor called my name, and I was shocked to

hear that I passed with flying colors. I walked out of that room that day

with a sense of accomplishment, which was something very unfamiliar

to me.

After hearing the two guys talking about the military, I started

thinking maybe that would be a good route for me as well. I was

guaranteed three hot's and a cot (meaning three meals and a bed.) I

walked to my mother's school that day to tell her the good news. I

actually passed my test, and now I was planning on going into the

military. The next morning I went to the recruiter's office and told him

Fire and Faith

I wanted to enlist. The recruiter told me I had to take another test and pass a physical. He handed me a book that I needed to study and sent me home. My plan was set. I was going to pass this test and go off to the military. That meant I did not have to deal with Bob ever again. I studied the book and before I knew it, it was time to go take the test. The recruiter drove me and a few other guys down to take the test. The test was long and I was not sure if I passed it, but I gave it all I had. The recruiter drove us back to the office. He told us to come back the next morning to get the physical out of the way. When I arrived the next morning, they completed my physical.

The doctor had us remove our clothing while he conducted the physical. The first thing the doctor noticed was the scars on my legs. He asked me about them, and I remembered my recruiter told me to tell him that they were just cuts that needed stitches. I was supposed to lie so I could pass the physical. The doctor said 'If it's all the same to you, I would like to take an x-ray." When the x-rays came back he saw the screws in my leg, and told me that I would be a liability. The doctor asked me for the truth and I told him that I was in a bad ATC wreck. He told that the Navy was not going to accept me. I went back to my recruiter's office that afternoon and told him I did not make it. He suggested that I try a different branch of the military. That day I tried the Marines, Army and Air force, and I could not get in any of them.

I walked home that day completely deflated. I knew that I was never going to hear the end of from Bob and I was right. He had nothing but bad things to say. At that point I had absolutely nothing left inside of me. My mom came home from work a few days later and told me about an art school in Phoenix, Arizona. She told me that there were recruiters looking for students at her work. She also told me that the recruiter was coming to our house that night to talk to me. I'd always enjoyed drawing, but I never thought that I would go to school for it.

When the recruiter showed up that night, he asked to see some of my drawings. Apparently my drawings were good enough for me to get into the school, and if I wanted to enroll, I could. I showed him one of my drawings, which was a rose. He immediately said that just a flower. I let him look at it again, and after looking at it long enough, he saw that there was a human face in the flower. He seemed excited and quickly asked me if I was ready to start. He explained that classes started in January, and the program was only a year long. I had three weeks before I would leave for Arizona. I thought that my mother would be taking me to this school to do all the registration and help get

me get set up.

Chapter 13

I had to find an apartment, and the school would be helping me to do that. The apartments near the school housed a lot of students that attended. I quickly realized that I would be doing all this alone. I got on an airplane, and was on my way to Arizona. I took a taxi from the airport to the school and found the office. I was placed in an apartment with a roommate whose name was Kevin. He was a pretty cool guy and we seemed to hit off right away. The first night we were in our apartment we talked about where we were from. We talked a little about who we were and where we were going.

As the night went on he asked me if I smoked weed. I told him yes, but it had been awhile. He pulled out a large bag, and we smoked most of it the first night. It was not long before we found other people that did the same thing. We were able to get weed all the time, and most of it was free. School started the following Monday and it was easy as it gets. All I had to do was draw. School became my second concern though, because I found that partying once again at the top of my list. The upcoming month was February and my birthday was the 8th. By this time, I had a large group of friends that also like to get high and we partied all the time. This time was going to be different though. I was turning seventeen, and this party was going to be huge.

The night of the party had come, and we had two kegs, five bottles of hard liquor, (tequila, vodka and Jack Daniels). We also had a variety of drugs: weed, cocaine, speed and acid. I had a little of everything that night. I drank way to much alcohol and I found myself the next morning in the bathtub soaked in my own vomit. When I walked out into the living room I found naked girls and half naked men lying on the floor. Everyone was still passed out. For the next three months this lifestyle became normal for me; partying all night, and not remembering a thing. In fact my motto used to be "If you can remember last night, you did not have a good time." We never had money for rent. I would call my grandparents and my mother for money all the time. It was not long before we were evicted out of that apartment complex for not paying rent and being too loud. We found another place to live in a different apartment complex, but it was in a crappy part of town. It was filled with prostitutes and drug dealers, but the rent was cheap.

I was still going to school and passing, but I was not really learning anything. I was just showing up with my drawings and somewhat paying attention in class. I guess that was good enough for this school.

Fire and Faith

Kevin and I ended up with another roommate and his name was Randy. Randy was a good guy and he lived above us, but he could not pay his rent either. So when he got booted out he moved in with us. Now there were three of us that could not pay rent. Having an extra roommate did not help with money but he did teach us how cook potatoes one-hundred different ways. Because we were always broke, the only thing we could afford was Top- Ramen and a bag of potatoes. We had potato soup, mashed potatoes, potato chips, potato fries, hash browns and baked potatoes. Randy was pretty good about making food. Randy and I started to become really good friends, and Kevin started showing signs of jealousy. Kevin stopped talking to us and eventually moved out.

Randy and I stayed together, and for the next five months partied enough to last a life time. Randy ended up meeting a guy that was a cocaine dealer, and that became our new drug of choice. We used to sell cocaine to support our ever-increasing habit. The more we sold for this guy the more we got. We used to bring the cocaine home and place it in a jar; we added a little water and baking soda to it and heated it up. The cocaine would dissolve and re-form into a rock. We would then take the rock and break it into pieces and smoke it. Randy and I would smoke enough to get twenty people high every night. Cocaine seemed to be the drug of choice with all the girls as well. There were

always at least three or four girls at our apartment every night. They

were only there to get high and Randy and I knew it. Our apartment

was a page right out of Sodom and Gomorra from the Holy Bible. I

knew why the girls were there, and I took advantage of that.

I remember one night Randy and I were actually alone in the

apartment, when there was a knock at the door. Randy and I scurried

around trying to hide all of drugs. When I opened the door, there was a

man and a women standing there with a clipboard in their hands. They

asked if Joey lived here and I responded with, "Who wants to know?"

They told me that they were from the free clinic, and that I needed to be

there first thing in the morning. I asked them why and what were they

talking about. They told me that I had slept with a girl that had

gonorrhea, and that it was in connection with aids. I asked how they

knew who I was sleeping with, and that said that she put me down on

her list. I was so pissed off that she knew she had this disease, and yet

she slept with me anyway. I asked them what I needed to do and the

reminded me to be at the clinic first thing in the morning. The next

morning I had Randy drive me down to the clinic. I was so freaked out.

I thought for sure my luck had finally run out. I had been through so

much and this is the way it was going to end, with aids?

Fire and Faith

When we got to the clinic I was so embarrassed to tell the lady

behind the counter why I was there. She told me to fill out the papers

and have seat. I waited for about a half an hour and they finally called

me in. The nurse asked a bunch of questions relating to sexually

transmitted diseases. The nurse asked if I had any symptoms yet and I

said no. The nurse asked me if I ever had a sexually transmitted

disease, and I told them no. She told me to take my clothes off, and

wait for the doctor to come in. I felt so weird taking my clothes off for

a man to come in and examine me. I had a sick feeling in my stomach.

When the doctor finally came in, he said "OK. Let's get started." (He

said it like it was a race or something!) He said this was going to be

very uncomfortable. He had a long piece of metal shaped much like a

pencil led. At the end of the metal, it was flattened out so it was wider.

He told me that he had to get a culture sample and there was only one

way to get it. (It looked like a hammerhead shark)! He had to push

that metal piece up inside of my penis. The pain was horrible. I just

wanted it over with. He said "If you think that hurt, wait until you get

the shot." I thought he was kidding. Then he had me turn around and

gave me penicillin shot right in my butt. Then I had to swallow about

twenty-five different pills, and then told me I could get dressed. He

also told me that I would get a phone call from the clinic in about three

days.

Fire and Faith

The next three days were absolute hell. I stayed by the phone

waiting to hear my doom. When the third day finally came I was

overwhelmed of the possibility of having aids. I was not sure if I should

call my mother or not. That was the first day I was sober since I got to

Arizona. The phone finally rang and they told me my test were

negative for gonorrhea, and any other sexually transmitted diseases.

Once again someone above was watching out for me, and I still did not

know it yet. When I got the news, I had Randy drive me down to the

clinic again to have a blood test. I wanted to be convinced that there

was not a problem. The results were the same. I was clean. You'd

think that a person going through that type of scare would want to start

making better choices and positive change. I believe in my situation

though, without even knowing it, I was on a path of self-destruction. I

was not actually thinking, 'Hey I want to destroy myself.' But I was

unconsciously on that path. There seemed to be no cap to the things I

did. As far as I was concerned, I was indestructible. I could do as

much drugs as I wanted. I had nothing to lose except myself, and that

did not mean much to me. I think that is why I continued to do drugs

into my adult years. I will talk about that in another chapter.

When I got the news that I was free of any disease, Randy and I

ordered as much cocaine as we could possibly get, and we had a massive party. We had people in the apartment that I had never seen before. Someone brought LSD, a hallucinogenic, also known as "acid". The first time a person does it, the most they do is laugh a lot. I had done this drug at least nine or ten times, so I was sure to hallucinate. When the party finally died down and people started leaving, Randy and I decided to take the acid. We started putting these acid dipped pieces of paper on our tongues and waited for about a half hour and then put another. By placing two of them at different times it makes the high much stronger. After about an hour we were flying high. I kept looking around the living room thinking it was a mess. So Randy and I decided to clean up. The apartment had never been that clean. It took us two hours to do it, but it was spotless. When we sat down we then looked around again and started asking each other questions.

The questions we were asking each other were odd ones. I asked Randy what he would do if someone walked in our and tried to rob us. He told me he would get up and beat the heck out of him. Then he asked me the same question. I paused for a moment and looked around the apartment. I looked at the baseball bat leaning against the wall by the front door. I quickly jumped up, and grabbed the aluminum bat and hit the coffee table over and over again, until it was just splinters on the

Fire and Faith

floor. Randy started laughing and grabbed the lamp of the end table and smashed it against the wall. I told Randy that if someone else came in, I would throw my knife at him. I had a straight-blade, boot knife, and I threw it at the front door and it stuck straight in. Randy and I did not stop there. We traded off the bat and knife, and we destroyed every piece of furniture in the place. The couch, television, coffee and end-tables, and completely destroyed the kitchen table and chairs. The apartment was a complete disaster. When we finished destroying everything and we caught our breath we said, "What are we going to do?" We had nothing but a mess.

The apartment complex we lived in offered furnished apartments. All the furniture we just destroyed was not even are own. Randy moved the curtains back and looked out the window. He said it was still dark outside, and we should go and throw all this away. I told him I had a better plan. I told him we should load all this mess up, and put it in a different apartment, and take the good furniture out and replace ours. Randy agreed, and so we loaded everything up, and replaced it all. We even grabbed an extra couch and another chair. By the time the sun came up we had a brand new apartment. After moving all of the furniture it was about 11:00 a.m., we decided to try and get some rest.

Fire and Faith

Randy was lying down on the new couch, and I was standing in the kitchen. I was telling Randy that the acid really did not do that much for me. He started laughing and said that he agreed. At the time I was leaning on the chair in the dining room, and it felt like it was pushing me. It was obvious that I was starting hallucinate. I told Randy that I was going to go and try to sleep it off. We had been up for twenty-four hours or more.

When I walked into my room, I remember looking at my closet doors. The doors were mirrors and when I walk up to them I touched them. I remember that it rippled like water when I touch the mirror. I knew I needed to get some rest. When I got into bed, I tried to close my eyes but it was hard not to look around my room. When I looked at my door in my room, I saw neon colored, geometric shapes floating through the air. I got up out of bed and went into the living room where Randy was. I sat on the other couch and told him that I could not sleep. Randy was wide awake as well. We stayed awake the rest of the day until we both finally fell asleep.

In the apartment upstairs lived an old man. I don't know if he really was old, but he looked it to me. He spent most of his adult life in prison, and he really did not like anyone. For some reason though he thought I was ok. He would come down stairs once in a while and talk

179

Fire and Faith

to me about how drugs were going to get me into trouble someday. He was a cool old man, and I am sure he was just trying to help me out. His name was Sunny and he did not party at all. He told me that if he got caught with drugs, he would have to go back to prison. Sonny was not even aloud to drink. He told me that if he even sneezed wrong, he would have to go back. He would tell me stories about his past, and it sounded a lot like mine. In fact, he used to tell me that I reminded him of himself when he was younger. He also told me that it would catch up with me sooner or later. He told me that everyone who does drugs, ends up getting sloppy. Meaning, that sooner or later everyone will either get caught or end up dead.

Randy and I grew our own marijuana in the apartment. Our plants were pretty good size, and there was always enough for us to get high every night. One of the plants that Randy was growing was not doing so well. It was only about a foot tall, but it was a little droopy. Randy figured it needed a little sun to perk it up. So Randy's bright idea was to put it out on the stairs, and let it have natural sunshine. I remember this day like it was yesterday. A friend of mine was sitting in the living room with me, and Randy was at the store. My friend Brian and I did not even know or see that the plant was sitting on the stairs, which lead to Sonny's apartment. The curtains and the window were open while Brian and I were watching television.

Sonny came home and was making his way up the stairs, when I heard him yell "What the heck is this?" I quickly stood up to make sure Sonny was ok, and right at that time the whole plant came flying through the open window of our apartment. He was so mad and screamed "What the heck is wrong with you guys?" I told him "It's not my plant, and that I had no idea that it was even out there." He said "That's it! You have had it now!" I went outside and said "Come on Sunny. I had no idea that was even out there!" He had no part of it, he was mad. Sonny said that if the police ever showed up for a random inspection, and saw the plant that he would be taken back to prison. He slammed the door behind himself and yelled "You all are going to get it now!"

Within about five minutes, I heard yelling in the parking lot out in front of our apartment. I looked out the front window of our apartment, and saw Randy outside with Sonny and a very large biker. This biker's nickname was "Smiley" and he was not 'smiley'. In fact, he was downright mad and aggressive. I went out the front door and yelled "Hey leave him alone!" That was a mistake, Smiley then turned to me. I saw a large pipe wrench in his hand. Sonny said "No, not him." But

Fire and Faith

Smiley was not listening. He came towards me swearing and swinging the wrench side to side. Smiley was about two feet in front of me, when he swung that wrench towards my head. I ducked down and the wrench missed me by inches. He actually hit the pole that was next to me and split the wood.

I turned and ran towards my apartment door. I grabbed the handle and turned it as fast as I could to get in. When I looked back, Smiley was right on my heels. I ran through the living room and could not figure out what I was going to do. I could either run to my bedroom or to the bathroom. Either way I was screwed, I had no weapons within reach, so I decided to turn and fight this giant of a man. This was definitely a seen from David and Goliath, but the difference was, I was not going to be able simply throw a stone and win. This man was a monster, and I lacked the strength from God. I will say however God was definitely looking out for me. At least I am here to write this story.

I turned quickly to face him head on, and he was right there. Before I could even put my hands up he had already hit me in the cheek. That blow to the face not only lifted me up off my feet and knocked into the bathtub, but broke my cheekbone. Everything started to go black. I was going to pass out. I remember seeing the wrench come towards my knees, and I moved them just in time. Then I saw his other hand

Fire and Faith

and reach down and pick me up by my t-shirt. That is when I realized the size difference between him and me.

At the time I was only seventeen and I stood five feet, ten inches. I was one-hundred forty-five pounds soaking wet. Smiley was six foot, seven inches tall, and weighed about two-hundred fifty pounds. He dragged me back out of the bathroom and toward the hallway. I figured at any moment Brian or Randy would show up to help me take down this big man. But, the front door was still stuck in the wall from when I'd fallen through it, and Brian was still standing in the same spot. Smiley let me go and started making his way to the front door. As Smiley walked passed Brian he hit Brian in the face and broke his glasses. I quickly ran over to Brian to help him up.

After making sure Brian was ok, I ran outside to check on Randy to see if he was ok. When I went out there, Randy was nowhere to be found. Randy's car was gone from the parking spot. I could not believe that he actually left. While I was outside, Smiley asked me if I wanted more. I just put my hand up and nodded my head no. I was completely surprised he did not come over and hit me again. Sonny was telling Smiley that he had hit the wrong guy, but Smiley did not care. I went back into the apartment to check on Brian, and that is when the pain set in on my face. I had been hit a lot in my life, but this

Fire and Faith

time was the hardest. I told Brian that I thought something was really
wrong with my face, because the pain was extreme.

After about an hour of the pain, I finally asked Brian if he could take
me to the doctor. On the way there to the doctor, Brian told me that I
needed to get out of that apartment. I told him that I did not want to
talk about it right then. I told him I was such pain that I could not even
think straight. When we got to the doctor's office they immediately
took an x-ray of my face and found that Smiley actually hit me hard
enough to break the cheek bone of my skull. I asked the doctor, "Well,
what do I do now?" The doctor kind of smiled, and told me that he
could not put a cast on my face. The doctor said I would just have to
deal with it until it healed. I think it was about two weeks before I
could put sunglasses on.

On the way back to our apartments Brian started back up about me
leaving. He also told me that I needed to stop doing the drugs, and that
I was a great guy, but when I was on drugs he hated to be around me.
One of the coolest things to me was that Brian did not do drugs. He
said that if I did not stop doing drugs, and move out that he would not
hang around with me anymore. Brian knew that I was up to about a
two-hundred dollar habit a day. He knew that my meth intake was
large and that I would probably have to go through withdrawals to get

Fire and Faith

off the drug. I asked Brian "Where would I go? I have no place to go."
He said "You could stay at my apartment until we got out of school." I
told him that I would think about it. I asked him to give me a day or
two to figure things out. What I was really saying was 'Let me party
for a couple more days', and then I will decide.

Brian was a great guy, and the most he did wrong, was having an
occasional beer. Brian's heart was definitely in the right place, but I
was not. I was all about being with girls, drugs and whatever I could
find to numb myself. That night I had been partying pretty hard, and I
ended up passing out. The people in my apartment could not wake me
up. They ended up calling Brian over and they got me back to his
apartment. Brian was able to get me to wake up, and he told me that if
I left that I was not allowed back. I told Brian that I was done with it
all. I was scared. It was the highest I had ever been.

I spent the next seven days in pure hell. My stomach was killing me
from not being able to have cocaine. I could not stay awake for more
than ten minutes at a time, before I would fall asleep for another few
hours. When I did wake up, and my stomach was not killing me, I
would eat sweets like cookies and candy. That was the only thing I
craved. The sweets kept me awake a little longer. I loved to drink milk

to wash down the junk food. Brian was very patient with me through all of it, and I did get through it.

We only had about three months left before we graduated. I spent the next three months sober. I learned a lot in school, but my drawing ability was horrible. I actually drew better high. Brian would tell you that I could not draw at all. All kidding aside, Brian and I did pretty well as roommates. After school we spent most of our time playing guitar together. Brian did well with everything he did. He had a great relationship with his parents. Brian talked to his parents every Friday night, and I was pretty envious of that relationship. I never showed that to him, or even told him that. He did ask me one night though if I needed the phone to call my parents, to tell them that graduation was coming. It was a pretty big deal; the school rented a big room at a fancy hotel. I told Brian, "They won't be at my graduation."

Graduation was close, and when I thought about it, the year had flown quickly. When I think of it now, I wish I could do all over again, (the school part, not the drugs.) I believed I missed a lot of material that was covered throughout the year. I believed the only reason I passed was because of my drawings. I got ready that morning, and put on the best clothes I had for the ceremony. Brian and got there a little early, so we could get a good seat up front. When I looked around the room there were many parents there to support their children. I kept thinking my mother or grandparents would sneak in and surprise me. But that did not happen. The ceremony ended, and Brian was leaving right afterward to go home. We said our goodbyes, and he told me to stay away from drugs. I told him that should not be a problem considering I was going to live at my grandparent's house that was in the middle of nowhere, so it was not like I could just run next door and buy them.

I would be staying at the apartment for a day or two until my grandparents drove down the mountain to get me. I planned on staying at their house for a little while. I guess Bob really did not want me back with my mother at the time. My grandparents showed up early the following morning and we loaded my stuff into the car. The trip back to their house was about an hour and a half. I can tell you that there is not a whole lot to do in Prescott, Arizona. In fact, it was really boring, unless you were retired. I spent the better part of five months there. The only thing I did was draw the whole time. I was trying to put together a portfolio for when I went back to California where my mother lived. While I was there I had my eighteenth birthday, and I finally went down to get my driver's license. I wanted to get this done before I went back to California only because I was convinced that if I didn't do it then, I would never get it. I figured Bob would somehow

get in the middle of it and prevent it from happening.

Chapter 14

Shortly after getting my license, I moved back to California. My grandmother was able to drive me back with all my stuff. I stayed with Bob and my mother while I looked for a job. During this time my mother helped me get my first car. It cost four-hundred dollars and it was a pile of garbage. I did not care though. It was mine, and it meant freedom. I loved the thought of working for the military. I figured if I could not be a soldier, maybe I could design for them. I really wanted to be an aircraft designer, or design different types of weapons. I guess I set my goals too high, because I heard the same from every company. Every place I applied, they all told me to come back when I got some experience. I always thought to myself, 'How can I get experience if no one will give me a chance?"

I quickly became discouraged and found myself losing interest in being a graphic artist. My problem was that I did not know how to deal with disappointment. The job I took after graduation was at a grocery store. I was starting to slip into my old ways. I noticed a very pretty girl and decided to ask her out. For me, it was all about having sex. Sex was all I wanted, and before I knew it, I was dating six different girls at the same time. I never cared about how they would feel after I

Fire and Faith

left them. I was only in it for my own self pleasure. Don't get me wrong, in my mind, (and the key word here is "mind," not "heart"), I loved all the girls I was with. I don't think I really knew what love was. I just knew if it felt good and saw the as precious I though it must be love. It was not long though before they figured it out that I was on the hunt for another set of girlfriends. A friend of mine recently told me that the definition of love is friendship on fire. I think that is a wonderful definition.

During this time I met a girl who truly adored. Her name was Shannon. She was everything I loved in a girl. She was very short, and I am a sucker for a short girl. I was outside washing my truck in front of my house when I saw this cute girl pass by on her scooter. She looked at me and I was definitely looking at her. She passed back by again, and I got in my truck and went after her. She pulled over and we talked for a bit and then I asked her out. I came by and met her parents first, and then we were off to go and get something to eat. The first date was great and I was looking forward to the next.

The next day I went by Shannon's house and her dad was out in the driveway working on his truck. His name was Ray. He was a great guy and we seemed to really hit it off. We ended up becoming best friends. We did everything together when Shannon and I were not together. I know that part of my friendship with Ray was about finding a dad. I obviously did not have a father figure, and part of me loved that about Ray. We did things that I thought a father and son would do. He taught me how to work on my truck and understand the mechanics of a vehicle. Shannon and I often went to dinner with her parents and did other fun things as well. When we went to amusement parks it was almost like double dating. The time we spent together seemed to be the best times of my life. I was actually content being with one girl. I truly loved her, and planned on marrying her.

I know that my parents and her parents knew this as well. Everyone that knew us thought that we would marry someday. One of the greatest things about her was that she would not give up her body to me. I tried, believe me, when I say, I tried. Shannon was such a wonderful kisser. She would make me like putty in her hands. We would be together, and our kissing would get pretty heated up, and I would make my move, but every time she would stop us. One of the most wonderful things she taught me was respect. The respect however was only for her. I still saw other girls as a target for my own pleasure. I saw all the women I dated as beautiful, but I lacked the respect for them. I figured if I was not hurt during the split up, why would they be hurt?

Fire and Faith

Shannon and I stayed together for about a year before our relationship started to die down. During this time, Shannon's dad and I were pretty close. Later in life I found out from Shannon one of the biggest reasons for our breakup was because of how close Ray and I were. I always thought that was a good thing. Ray and I often took trips together and would go to Hollywood and cruise Hollywood Boulevard. We were like two best friends acting like kids. I was always at their house, even when Shannon wasn't there. We would always be in the driveway working on our trucks and across the street from Shannon's house was another girl that I had my on. Every once in a while she would come across the street and talk to Shannon's parents. Her name was Debbie and she was beautiful. I did not know it at the time, but she would be my future wife.

I had a problem with keeping my social life separate from my work life. I was starting to go downhill fast. I could not keep a job for anything. I seemed to have problems with authority. I quickly lost the job at the grocery store. I went through five more jobs before I took a job working in a juice factory. Bob came in my room one night, and told me I had one month to get out of the house. He told me that I needed to get my own apartment as soon as possible and that I had been there long enough. I guess six months was "long enough". During this time, I was making pretty good money at the juice factory, and I decided to purchase a stereo receiver, and a cd player that would later be used in my new apartment. I couldn't let Bob know I had it though. He would completely flip out knowing that I spent some of my own money on myself, not to mention he hated anything that had to do with my music.

Right about the time I was to get my apartment I was laid off from my job. I never told the apartment complex for two reasons. The first reason was because I had already signed the lease two weeks before, and if I told them, I would have lost my apartment. The second reason and this is the most important one, Bob was not going to let me stay at the house. My best chance was to move into my apartment and pray that I found a job in time. For the next couple of days I looked for work and I finally found a job at a cable company. The money was not near enough to pay my bills. Once again, I had to rely on my grandparents to send me money to help pay the rent. My mother was also there to help as well. The problem with that was I was not allowed to say anything about the financial help in front of Bob. Bob was not going to help me in anyway.

Shannon and I finally came to end with our relationship and it was not long before I was back   in the mode of "love 'em, and leave

Fire and Faith

'em". I only was after getting sex with as many girls as I could. That is how I felt love. It seemed to at the time that was the only way to fill the void, but the truth is, and I did not know it, was that God was the only thing that could fill that void. I know it was wrong, but that is how I lived. I would get what I could from them, and then move on. I was so mixed up in the arena of love that I had no idea of the destruction I was causing in the lives of the girls I was with.

Even after Shannon and I broke up, I was still going over to her house and I would hang out with Ray. He and I would still work on our trucks and do stuff together. During this time, I started to see Debbie outside working in the front yard. I used to think to myself, "Wow, just one time with her would be great." I would always come back to my senses and realize that she did not live alone. She shared a house with a guy. A guy I assumed was her boyfriend. I remember one night I was talking to Ray, and I asked him if he knew what was going on with Debbie and the guy she lived with. Ray told me that he thought that their relationship was only plutonic. Ray thought they just bought the house that they lived in for an investment, and that there was nothing going on between them. Debbie was older than me by 4 years, and that for some reason made me a little nervous about asking her out. I mean seriously, she owned her own house and worked in

Fire and Faith

downtown Los Angeles on the fifty-second floor of a tall sky scraper. "What chance did I have besides the bad boy attitude?

I guess it was enough though. I planned on asking her out right after I left Ray's house. They lived on a cul-de-sac, and I had to pass her house on the way out. I had no idea what I was going to say to her. The only thing I had going for an opening conversation was the fact Debbie and I had identical trucks. They were the same year, make, model and color. The only thing that was different was she had a shell for the back of the bed of the truck. Not quite a camper shell, more like a snug top. I noticed the top had been removed, so I used this as my conversation starter. I pulled in front of her house and asked where the top was and she looked in her garage. The top was in plain sight, and I think she knew where I was trying to go with the conversation at that point. Debbie walked over to my truck, and put her head in through my passenger window, and asked if I would like to go to a concert sometime. Of course I agreed, and that was the start of our relationship. This was not going to be a pleasure trip though, in the beginning it was, but it soon turned somewhat ugly.

Chapter 15

Debbie was living with a guy that she used to date, and was not until sometime later that I found out that she the relationship was abusive. For now, I just knew that we were going on our first date soon and I needed to make some money quick. I was still working at that cable company and they did not pay enough for me to take Debbie to a nice place. I remember it was a late Friday afternoon and our first date was later that evening. Just by chance I was on my way back to the shop when I saw a car had driven off the road. I pulled over with my partner from work to make sure he was ok.

When we approached his vehicle we realized that he was stuck in the mud just off the freeway. I asked my partner to give me a hand, and we pushed the care out to get him back on the road. We pushed with everything we had in us, and we finally got him out onto the road. My partner and I waved to him, and got back into the company truck. As we were driving away the man sped up to where we were and flagged us to pull over. When we pulled over, the man's arm was up through his sunroof of his car. He had what looked like money in his hands and as I reached over to grab it I looked into his car. He had stacks of hundred dollar bills on the passenger seat. There must have been at least fifty or sixty thousand dollars on the seat. I took the money from his hand and realized he had handed us two hundred dollars. There was a hundred for me, and a hundred for my partner. I told my partner how I'd seen the money on the seat and told him that I wanted to follow him and jump him. In fact, I told him if I'd been alone, I would have. My partner told me that he did not want to do that, so we got off the freeway and returned to work.

With the money I just got from the man we rescued on the freeway I had enough for my first date with Debbie. I took her to decent restaurant that night and we seemed to hit it off. I was more interested at the time to get in her pants, and I am sure she knew that. The first date went very smooth and I asked her if she would like to get together the next night, and she agreed. I went home that night and could not wait to see her again. When the next day came around I decided that it would great to clean my apartment. I did not have much in it, so it was rather simple to clean. I had one oversized chair in the living room that Ray gave me. I also had my nice stereo and crappy television and one queen sized bed. That was all I needed. As the day came to an end, I realized I had no food in the apartment. My pantry was filled with pop-tarts and candy corn. My fridge had coke and milk. That was my diet.

Fire and Faith

absolutely needed to use the phone that I could walk to the pay-phone
in the apartment complex.

The weekend soon came, and I thought it would be nice if we went
to my mother's house and told her that I was going to be married in a
year. We went my mother's house to introduce her and make the
announcement. When we walked in, Bob was in his chair watching the
game on television, and my mother was standing at the door asking us
to come in. We walked into the house and I introduced Debbie to my
mother and then to Bob. Bob just sat in chair and barely turned his
head to even look at her. I was so mad at Bob for being such a jerk.
Our plan was not to stay too long. I told my mother that we were going
to be married in about a year, and she was very happy. My mother was
actually starting to cry with happiness. My mother asked us if we
would stay for dinner and we did. After dinner Deb and I helped my
mother clean up and then we went home.

Our relationship started to have problems shortly after getting
together. I quickly found out that she was a very possessive and
jealous girl. I could not even go and visit my old friends, and a trip to
the store for cigarettes was like pulling teeth. Debbie was always afraid
that I would meet another girl in that short period of time and start
dating them. In her defense though, her last boyfriend was cheating on

her at every possible moment. So it made it very difficult for her trust anyone. At the time however, I thought that this was not a good enough excuse. This felt too much like work to me and I was not prepared to do it. I felt that she should trust me no matter what. I mean come on; she did ask me to marry her. I was actually starting to get completely disgusted with her, and I was finding it difficult to stay committed to her. I was being blamed so much for cheating that I actually started to believe I was that kind of guy. The problem I was faced with however was I believed that if I committed to marriage that I would only marry once so no matter what I would not split up.

On top of the distrust she had for me, I had my own problems. I could not keep a job to save my life. Debbie ended up taking on all the bills, and I was unemployed more than I was working. Our relationship continued to suffer along the way. We would fight so horribly that we would call each other nasty names, and it seemed our love for each other turned into "love to hate." Probably most people in their right mind would have walked away from this and split up. I had so many friends telling me to move on and forget about the relationship. Our fights were so bad that I was on the brink of wanting to hit her. To be perfectly honest, I don't know why we stayed with each other. Our fights were constant and an everyday occurrence. This lasted for

Fire and Faith

months and months. The years passed by and our fights were not as often, but they were incredibly horrible when they did happen. We did have some good times in the mix of all this. The problem was that we were both screwed up, and had our own problems and baggage that we were trying to sort through.

We ended up leaving California and moved to Arizona together. My mother and Bob had already moved to Arizona about six months prior. My aunt and uncle had already been in Arizona for about fifteen years as well. My aunt found us a place to rent before we came out. It was in a crappy part of town, but Debbie and I had lived in worse conditions. I tried to start up a landscape company, and it was all we could do to keep food in the house. It was really tough, and we had a hard time being able to even put dinner on the table. We would work together all day in heat, and had just enough money for crackers and cheese for dinner. Between the fighting and lack of money and food my I started developing a serious attitude or temper problem.

Debbie and I worked in 120 degree weather and barley made anything. One day I was in the front yard washing my truck, when this guy in his car was going about 60 miles an hour down the street. I looked up and flicked the hose at him and said, "Slow down!" At that point he slammed on the brakes and came to a screeching halt. He

Fire and Faith

jumped out of the car and pointed a rifle at me across his hood of the

car. I do not know what he was thinking, but this was not the first time

I had a gun pointed at me. This did not bother me at all and I continue

to walk towards him yelling at him to go ahead and pull the trigger. I

screamed it at him, "Go ahead punk pull the trigger you coward!" As I

got closer to the car with 10 feet, he yelled out, "You aren't worth it!"

He then got back into his car and drove away. As I turned and went

back to the house, I noticed the entire neighborhood outside staring at

me. They were asking if they should call the cops and I told them no. I

think they all thought I was crazy or something.

Debbie and I stayed there as long as we could to try to make money,

but it seemed to be a never ending battle. We never had money for

anything, and things were getting pretty bad. Every once in a while we

hit a big payday, but all that had to go to past due bills. On a good

night we had grilled cheese sandwiches and tomato soup. We could not

even pay the rent where we lived, and it was not long before we had to

move out. I ended up trading my services to be able to pay some kind

of rent back to the landlord. I remember I put a new sprinkler system

in the front yard for him, just so we could be even.

During this time I had been in touch with my father. It was a few

phone calls during the weekends. We had talked a couple of times

Fire and Faith

about Debbie and me moving to the Carolinas where he was living.

Debbie and I just could not find work where we were at, and I decided

that we should move out to where my father lived and start a new life

together. I went to my mother to tell her about us leaving. She did not

want us to go. We were not making it there, and we had to change

something. My phone calls to my father helped us understand things

were different now that I was all grown up and I did not have to live

with him. We figured we should try and get to know one another. No

matter what happened between my father and me, it had to be better

than what Debbie and I were doing then.

My grandparent's gave Debbie and me a thousand dollars and my

mother did the same. The first thing we did was get something to eat

together. That was the richest we had been in a long time. We left in

early August, and drove cross-country in a moving truck. We actually

had a great time together. We drove long hours, traveled through many

storms along the way. We depended on each other, and that was

something we were not used to doing. I believe between living in

Arizona and the trip to the Carolinas, we became pretty close. We were

going to a place where neither one of us knew anyone. The trip out

there was major culture shock for us.

Fire and Faith

My father's new wife found Debbie and me a place to rent, while

my father got me an interview at the distribution center. He was able to

get me an interview, and the rest was up to me. The house we rented

was in Waterloo, South Carolina. This was a whole different

experience for the both us. The house was alongside the railroad tracks

and was about twenty-two miles from the grocery store. We moved our

things in, and I went to the distribution center to go and apply for a job.

I was fortunate and got a job immediately.

My first day at work was one I will never forget. I had a real

hard time understanding anyone that worked there. Their accents were

so thick, that it was difficult for me to understand what they were

saying. The worst part to me however, was that the white people

separated themselves from the colored people. During our lunch breaks

the whole company shut down, which meant everyone ate lunch at the

same time in the cafeteria. When I walked in to get my lunch, I noticed

that the white people sat on one side and the colored people sat on the

other side. I had never seen this behavior before. I was confused. I sat

down at a table by myself and was quickly joined by other white

people. They were asking me all kinds of questions, and telling me all

kinds of stories. But, I could not understand a thing they said due to

Fire and Faith

their southern accents. What I did notice was that the colored people

were having fun laying checkers.

The next at work, I decided to sit on the other side and play

checkers. Everyone in the place was staring at me. I have to admit

having two hundred white people staring at me with hate was pretty

intimidating. It did not matter to me though. I was used to the

intimidation, and I really did not care. I enjoyed my lunch everyday

playing checkers. Within three months I started to notice that the lunch

tables were starting to mix in color. The hate was starting to go away,

and all the credit goes to a game of checkers. I quickly worked my way

up in the company. This job for me was perfect. Everything came

really easy, and the work seemed almost second nature to me. I earned

three commendations during the time I was there. By the time I left,

everyone sat with everyone

Debbie took a job at the local pizza place in town and we were (for

the first time) somewhat happy. Everyone that Debbie worked with

thought she was the greatest. Our relationship was one like when a

brother and sister don't get along. Meaning if you have two siblings

not getting along, you place them in a room together until they figure

out how to be nice to each other, and get along. Debbie and I did very

well during our time together in the south. As for my father, I did not see him very often. He was still a truck driver and he was gone most of the time. During our time there, he did tell Debbie that he could not figure out why I wanted a relationship with him. He told her that he treated me so bad when I was a boy, and could not understand why I wanted to be near him.

Debbie and I made it a year before we were on our way back to Arizona. My grandparents ended up calling us up, and said that my great aunt had left some money to me in her will. My grandparents told us that they had used the money to have a house built in Arizona, and that we needed to move back. I did not know it yet, but this would be one of the worst decisions of my life! I applied for a transfer within the company, and I was fortunate that I got it. My employer gave me two weeks to make the move, and then I start back to work. I was excited to think that my life seemed to be improving. My relationship and my career seemed to be going great. Everyone I worked with at the distribution center gave my wife and me a going away party. We had a wonderful time. My father even showed up to this party. The next day was tearful for my wife and me, because we really enjoyed living there. After packing the twenty six foot moving truck once again, my wife and I were on the way to our new home and life.

Fire and Faith

We returned to Arizona and the trip seemed to take forever. In fact, it seemed to take longer getting home than it did getting to the Carolinas. On our way we home we stopped at a rest area. I was very tired and I decided to get a little sleep while I was there. I had been driving all day and most of the night, and I was getting very sleepy. I told Debbie that we needed a couple of hours of sleep. I must not have turned the headlights off, because when we woke it was pitch-black outside and we could not start the truck. The battery was dead and I had no way of starting the truck. Fortunately a highway patrolman showed up and was able to give us a jump start. Once we got the truck started we were on our way. We ended up in the mountains of Arizona late that afternoon. I remember we were going up a very steep hill and truck stopped moving forward and began to roll backwards. We got the truck safely parked alongside the freeway and called for repairs. The trucking company sent out a tow truck and towed us all the way back to our new home.

When we arrived to our new house we were exhausted. My grandparents were standing out in front of the new house with the key in their hand. Debbie and I were excited to get in our new home. We'd just had a great year together, and we figured that we were going to have a great future there in our new home. My grandparents proudly showed us our new home. They showed us all the wonderful features of our home. Then they told us that the house was on a fifteen year loan and not a thirty year loan. I asked them how much my house payment was going be and they told us. I freaked out! I mean I could not believe that the payment was so high. Our rent in South Carolina had been three-hundred fifty dollars a month. I asked why they did not get a thirty year loan because the house payment would have been much lower. My grandparents told me that it would be ok; that they would pay two hundred dollars a month toward the mortgage until we were on our feet. I told them that I was not even sure what my income was going to be at my new job, and that Debbie did not even have a job yet.

Sadly, what we didn't plan on was the fact that our income in Arizona would be far less than it had been in South Carolina. Our mortgage had literally doubled, and our utility bills had more than tripled! I knew that Debbie could find a job anywhere; that was not a problem. She was the most marketable person I knew. I told my grandparents I would have to talk with them after I got to my new job. They told us that it did not matter, that they would pay whatever the difference was. We spent the next week settling into the new house. Debbie and I had fun setting up our house. It was a great feeling to

Fire and Faith

know that we did not have to move anytime soon. For the first time,

with the exception of the Carolinas, it seemed that our life was going in

the right direction. We were actually enjoying each other's company.

Debbie and I actually talked about maybe having a child. We had a

new three bedroom home, and maybe after six years together it was

time to finally have a child. The last time we'd talked about kids was

when we'd first gotten together and we never talked about again until

that day.

I had to start work at the new distribution center. I was a little

nervous about going into a new job. It was actually the same job for

the same company, but it was a different facility. When I started it was

as if I was a new employee. They started me unloading trucks by hand

again, and all my forklift licensing was removed from me. The

company told me that I had to start all over again and work my way

back up. I was discouraged, and went to the personnel department to

find out if my situation could be corrected. They told me that there was

nothing that they could do for me. I inquired about the dollar an hour

raise I was promised, and they explained that this was Arizona, a right

to work state, and the increase in South Carolina, didn't apply. I asked

them about the three commendations in my personnel file, and he

literally threw my file into the garbage can. I could not believe what I

Fire and Faith

had just witnessed. They again reminded me that if I wanted to keep my job that I should get back to work.

I needed the job, so I returned back to my area and started working. This distribution center was nothing like the one I had come from. I could not believe that one center could operate so differently than the other. When I went home that night, Debbie told me not to worry about it. She told that I would do fine, and prove to them that I could do the job. She reminded me how well I did at the other center, and she said I would do it again. The fact remained that I felt that I shouldn't have to prove myself again. They should have honored the commitment that was made to me in South Carolina. I began feeling as if they owed me something. What I should have done was keep a positive attitude, smile and work my tail off, proving that I was worthy of what my file said.

I was having a hard time keeping up with the ever increasing production. At the time I was looking for anything that could help me get the job done. But, I had a seriously bad attitude towards the company, and I was starting to not care. I felt like everything was starting to slip away from me all at once. I felt as if I had no control over my future. I found myself hanging out with crew members that were on the rough side, and they were also the fastest at their jobs.

Fire and Faith

Their production was perfect every day, and I could not figure out how they were doing it. I remember one day, I asked one of my buddies how their production was so high. His name was Darrin, and he had the answer for me.

He asked me if I had ever done meth before. I did not want to seem like I was uncool, and I had done it before anyway. One might even say that I was a veteran user of meth. He kind of smiled and told me to go to the back of trailer and he would give me some. He told me that this meth was absolutely better than anything that had ever been made. He told me it was called lemon-drop. I had to say that he was right. It was so powerful! The name lemon-drop came from the lemony after taste. I immediately snorted a really big line, and felt the drug burn its way up my nose. Within minutes I felt it run down the back of my throat making its way to my stomach. I felt my heart begin to race, and my jaw started to clench. I felt a massive rush of energy throughout my body as the drug burned its way into my bloodstream. I went back to work, and I unloaded seven trucks that night setting a new company record.

When employees finished their production for the day, he or she usually had free time, or down time. The combination of using drugs and having down time was a window for me to get into trouble. Even

Fire and Faith

though I was doing well as far as production went, I still had ill feelings towards the company. Darrin and I would be the first ones finished with all of our work, and we would get on the forklifts and go to the backside of the warehouse and screw around. We would take broom sticks and basically joust each other as we past one another. On one particular evening we got a little carried away. We ended up making paper hats that looked like a soldier's armor. Now just to let everyone know, I was a lot of things, but I was never a racist. When Darrin and I were out in the isles of the warehouse jousting, we were caught by a man of color. He immediately went and reported what we were doing, and soon after we were called to the office. I figured that it would be a slap on the wrist, but when I found out they were firing us for gross discrimination, I was shocked. They actually thought that my paper hat represented the KKK. I could not believe what was happening. How stupid was that! In fact I actually thought that the prejudice was in their court for actually labeling me as a racist.

I went home that evening and had to tell Debbie that I had just been fired, and in my mind this was not going to be easy. Debbie had a job already working for a car dealership, but the pay was low. The bright spot in this disaster was that I knew how to work on cars, and I was able to get a job at the same place as my wife. This job was good, but again the pay was low as well. I had to explain to my grandmother that we would be short on money for bills, and asked her if she could still make up the difference in the mortgage only until we got a raise and then we would resume the payments. (Again, it would not have had a problem if the mortgage had been for thirty years). The house payment would have been cut in half. We had only been at the new house five months by this time, and we really did not want to lose it. My grandmother agreed that they would be able to help, and it was not going to be a problem.

Chapter 16

Everything seemed to be going pretty good for us. We had started

landscaping the front yard a little bit and started making it our home.

We'd also decided to have a child. Debbie was pregnant on the first

try, and I was extremely happy, but I had a hard time showing it. My

personal fears of the kind of a father I would be got in the way. I was

afraid that when the baby was born, a switch would flip inside me, and

I would become some kind of monster. I often hoped that I would not

become a tyrant like every other man from my past. The pregnancy did

not last long before Debbie had a miscarriage.

For Debbie this was huge and had a serious impact on her. It was

devastating to her and sadly enough, I did not feel as bad. In fact, I left

that night to go and party with my cousin, instead of staying home with

her. What a jerk I was, and I was so insensitive. But to be truthful, I

did not know how to deal with it. If I could only go back in time, and

stay with her in her time of need, I would. I was so selfish, and if I

were that selfish then, what made me think I would be any better with a

child. The next day we went the doctor to have her checked out. The

doctor told her that she did have a miscarriage for reasons unknown.

He told us that we should probably wait at least 3 months before trying

again for another child. We went home, and about a month later, we
tried again. We were pregnant again! We continued to go to work, and
do our best to get things ready for when the baby came. I started
painting our baby's room with Disney characters.

I guess I would have to say, that it did not really hit me that she was
pregnant until she started showing. We decided that we would not find
out the sex of the child because we wanted it to be a surprise. So we
planned on buying everything in neutral colors. Debbie and I were
going to be parents, and we realized that we still needed to get married.
The last time we said we were going to be married was cancelled. We
hadn't been getting along, and both her parents had been diagnosed
with cancer, and we used that as the excuse to postpone the marriage.

During this time I was still using meth on occasion, but in my mind
it was not a problem yet. I would work in our garage on the weekends
trying to get some work benches built. Our neighborhood was still in
the process of being built, and a lot of lumber was being thrown away.
This was an opportunity for me to save some money. My neighbor,
another friend of mine and I decided to go out one night and get all the
lumber that was being thrown away. Most of the construction workers
on the site did not care that we were taking the wood because it was
scrap in the dumpster.

Fire and Faith

We went out sometime after dinner just as it was getting dark. We walked to the street just behind our house and I started taking the some of the scrap out of the dumpster. I was not paying attention to my neighbor who had actually entered one of the homes nearby being built. He was stupid enough to go inside and start removing the interior doors. Just about the time he came out with the first door, a police officer pulled up. He asked what we were doing, and I told him that I was collecting scrap wood for a work bench in my garage. Then another officer pulled up, and they separated all of us and questioned us once again. I told the officer that I was only there to get getting scrap wood from the dumpster. It did not seem to matter what I said, we were handcuffed and placed in the cop car. My wife saw the siren lights from a window and walked around the corner to where we were. The police told my wife that I was being arrested and was being taken to the police station. The police officer was pretty decent though, he allowed her to give me a kiss before they took me away.

Our first stop was at a police transfer station. Then we were put into a van and brought to another police station. It was at this station, we were booked. They took our finger prints and pictures, and the officer doing all of this was very nice. I know that sounds weird, but I felt I had done nothing wrong, and I believed that everything would be

Fire and Faith

cleared up soon. While I was being fingerprinted, I kept telling the officer in a joking manner that, I did not want to be put in the cell with a guy named "Bubba." It was a joke and the humor was much needed in this situation. They placed my two friends and me in a cell that had a few other guys in it. It was late at night and almost everyone was asleep. I got up into one of the bunks and tried to get some sleep, when I heard one of my friends crying on the phone with his wife. I could not believe it! I thought to myself that he was going to get our butts kicked. I said to him "Shut up and suck it up."

We were there for about two hours before we were transferred again to the Phoenix police department. This is what most people in Arizona call the "shoe". The name comes from the booking process. When a person first gets to the jail house, they start out in processing. This is where I was searched again for weapons and drugs. I was fingerprinted again and placed into the first cell. Then, from that cell we were moved from one cell to the next as the time drew closer to our court appearance. There are a total of five cells if my memory serves me right. When we reached the final cell, the next step is making a court appearance to make a plea. I was coming down off of meth, and was very sleepy. The only thing I wanted to do was sleep. I was placed into the first cell with my friends and about fifteen other guys.

Fire and Faith

One guy in the cell was determined to keep me from sleeping. As I climbed my way up into the top bunk, he kept poking me in the back, asking me "What are you in for?" I told him that if he poked me in the back one more time I was going to break his arm. He stepped back and told me that I could not talk to him that way and became enraged. Right about the time I rolled over to get down from the bunk he yelled, "You can't talk to me like I am a nigger!" I chuckled because I'd just made friends with the very large black man named Bubba at the other jail house. Bubba was transferred with the rest of us, and he was sitting in the cell with us. As I started to climb down off my bunk, Bubba looked at me and put his hand up and said "Lay back down Joe, I got this." Let's just put it this way, the man that yelled the "N" word needed medical attention after Bubba was finished.

After all the excitement was over I started to fall asleep. I don't even know how long I was sleeping, but when I woke, all the people I was with were now four cells ahead of me, including my so-called friends. I could not believe they'd left me behind. They could have at least woken me up. This put me way behind for my court appearance. I had no idea what time it was. The only thing I did know was that they were serving breakfast.

Fire and Faith

have to make a connection with her. In fact, I would build anything in the garage to avoid going in the house.

Eventually I gave in and married her. It is not that she was wrong for me. To be honest, there is no one in the world that would have put up with what I was about to do for the next seven years. Debbie and I got married at the court house. We did not have any money, and this was the cheapest way out. I will never forget the day we got married. Debbie walked into the courtroom and I followed her in. The judge saw Debbie and recognized her because he'd had his car serviced at the dealership she worked at. Keep in mind, my wife to be was eight and a half months pregnant and really big at the time.

As we entered the court room, Debbie entered first, and unable to see me behind her. When I came out from behind Debbie, he put his head down in disbelief. He asked her, "Is this the man you are marrying? And then, he asked her "Do you know who you are marrying?" I was shocked to realize that this was the same judge that I had been in front of before, for all the trouble I had ever been in. At the end, he smiled at me and said, "I have sentenced you before, and now I am sentencing you for life." Debbie and I were now husband and wife. It was just three weeks before the baby was due.

Chapter 17

I will never forget the day. It was February 6th 1996, and our first born child came into the world. I was actually sober, but I did have the flu. I was in the delivery room with my wife as she delivered the best thing in my life to me so far. I know a lot of men may dis-agree with me, but I feel it is the most incredible and beautiful wonder from God. The birth of a child is very precious. Our first child was a girl. She was the most beautiful thing I had ever seen. When the doctor handed her to me, I felt like a giant in a world filled with tiny flowers. That day, I learned what it means to be strong. Later, I heard from a friend of mine that a man had to be tender to be strong; meaning a man requires controlled strength to hold something so delicate. We spent just twenty four hours at the hospital before they discharged us. When we did finally get to leave, I drove twenty miles an hour all the way home. I was so cautious of bumps, so afraid of disturbing our precious "cargo". That wonderful part was the love I had for my daughter. I hope someday she will read this and realize that she makes my heart beat.

We arrived home and went through all the things that new parents go through: dirty diapers and crying. I reflected on my own past and wondered what was so different about me when I was a baby. For the

Fire and Faith

life of me I could not imagine hurting or hitting such a precious gift.

Why would anyone want to hurt me? We continued to watch this

blessing grow each day. My wife and I were enriched by our love for

this child. For the life of me, I still cannot figure out why I continued

to use drugs during this time. I am not sure if I was scared to be

attached, or if I had become accustomed to feeling of being high. I

think it was a combination of both. Don't get me wrong I loved to be

near my daughter. In fact everyone said that, I was so good to my kids

since most people who do drugs are never there for their children.

I believe that I was so afraid of everything that might happen that I

chose drugs because that fear was not present while I was high. As

time went on, my fear became my addiction. I was able to hide the

drugs for a while. I'd gained thirty pounds during the pregnancy, so for

me to lose weight was not really noticeable. I was still able to function

at work and in the home for the most part. However, Debbie and I

were not making enough money to be able to afford the home we were

in and the baby. My grandparents said they would help with the

monthly bills for the first two years. Unfortunately this did not happen.

Six months after the baby was born, we had to ask for monetary help

again. This time, they made a decision without us. They put the house

on the market and when we came home from work, there was a for sale

Fire and Faith

sign in our front yard. After a heated debate, they gave us two thousand dollars to find a place to live. I was so upset that the money originally used as a down payment on the house was my money from my great aunts inheritance, and I was not getting it back. I started to feel like a failure.

I believe that failure was one of the reasons that drove me deeper into my soon-to-be addiction. I felt like I was robbed from what was mine, and there was not a thing I could do about it. I know now that I was wrong about how I felt, but at the time that is where I was at mentally. I blamed everyone but, myself for what went wrong. I did not take any ownership for what was happening, including my drug problems. We rented a house that was somewhat decent and, we had Jimmy move in to help pay the bills. That decision was not good considering we were getting high on a daily basis now. My original rule that I only got high on Friday and Saturday nights and never during the work week changed drastically. My new rule was that I could get high every day, as long as I did not do it at work. It is very clear that the addiction was starting to set in.

I also maintained a rule that I would not be high around family members, at least not really high. I did not want them to notice anything different about me. The only thing noticeable was my weight

227

Fire and Faith

loss, and even that was easily covered by lies. I told everyone that I

was exercising. In the beginning everyone in my family said I was

starting to look really good. To be honest all the compliments left me

feeling pretty good, even though I was doing drugs to get that way. In

fact, I actually started to forget that the drugs were taking and the

weight off. I was also starting to justify the drug by the weight loss.

That did not last for too long though. Soon, my habit had brought my

weight to a point where everyone became concerned. I went from two-

hundred thirty pounds to one-hundred eight five pounds in a three

month period.

There was another problem starting to set in with my habit. My

relationship with Debbie was starting to suffer. We started fighting a

lot more often and the arguments were getting pretty severe. My life

was slowly becoming about the drug. When I had a lot of meth I was

happy and easy to get along with. I knew that I could simply go

outside in my garage and get high and everything was back to normal.

The problem was keeping enough money to get high. I started taking

money from my pay-checks to cover the cost of my drugs. I was never

home on time from work. My wife was starting to question me about

the shortage of money and where I was at. I always had an excuse as to

where I'd been. I explained my checks were shorted because my hours

Fire and Faith

were cut at work. I know she did not believe me, and we would fight about it often. My twenty dollars habit on weekends turned into twenty dollars a day.

It was not long before I ended up losing my job and forced to find another one. We ended up losing the house we were in. I found another home that was even worse than the one we just left. When you are high all the time, you don't really notice the direction you are moving in. In other words, I had a beautiful family, and it was slowly falling away. At that point in our relationship, I told Debbie that it would be best if she moved out. Debbie and I separated on our 1st year anniversary. She and our daughter moved in with my mom and Bob. Debbie was not happy with this decision, but I made it sound so convincing that she really did not have a choice.

Debbie would come by and bring my daughter to visit me every night for about an hour or so. The only thing I could do was look at my beautiful daughter and cry. I knew what I was doing. I knew that I was destroying my relationship with my daughter as well as my wife, but I could not get past the thought of being high. I literally could not help myself. I never told that to Debbie at the time. We were separated just about two months when Debbie and I talked about having her and the

Fire and Faith

baby moving back in. We agreed that it would be best for us all. Previously, I'd go to the garage and get high.

Then I graduated to getting high in the house when no one was home. Even after I lost my second job, I still found ways to getting money for my drugs. The sickening part was that my daughter stayed home with me because we could not afford daycare. During the days she was home with me, I went outside to get high so I would not be around her. She was about two or three years old at the time, and I would wait for her to go down for her nap, so I could go outside to get high.

On the days when I did not have any drugs I still was not there for my daughter mentally. I would fall asleep on the couch all the time. After being high for so long, my body would literally just shut down. I could not keep my eyes open. I would compare it to taking a bunch of sleeping pills, and then try and stay awake and fight the urge to sleep. It was an impossible task. I was a horrible father to my baby and a horrible husband to my wife.

I still had jimmy living with us, and he was getting ready to move into one of our drug dealer's house. Before Debbie moved back in I told myself that I was going to quit drugs and get clean. I actually thought I could accomplish this task on my own and in secret. I had to get clean, and in order to accomplish this I had to sleep. I used to call this "the big sleep." I would literally sleep for four to six days and only wake up long enough to go to the bathroom and eat.

About the fifth or sixth day I was able to get up and walk around. I called this my "sunshine day." I tried hard not to fall back into the drug world, but it was impossible considering I still hung around the same people. I managed to stay clean for a couple of months. During this time Debbie and I decided to have another baby. I truly had good intentions about staying clean and getting my life back together. I remember Debbie came home and she broke the news to me that she was pregnant. I did not know what to do. I was struggling so hard with my addiction that it was robbing all the joy that came my way. More importantly, the joy was being robbed from my wife. The sad part was I would get so down on myself about it that it seemed the only thing that got me out was being high. It was a vicious cycle that never seemed to end.

It was not long before I was sitting in a dealer's apartment and getting high again. Money was still a big problem. I took a part time job delivering pizzas at night, and was able to take my tips to buy the drugs that I needed. When I came home, I would tell my wife that it had been a slow night. I had to change it up on occasion. I did not want anyone wondering what was going on. I know now that she knew that I was not bringing all my money home. But at the time she believed I was cheating on her. I was in a way though, because of my dishonesty. After a while I started slipping up. What I tried so hard to hide started showing up, and my wife began to get suspicious.

As I mentioned previously, there are different means to use meth, it can be smoke, sniffed, eaten or injected intravenously, or some cases meth can be diluted in water and place in a baster then pushed into butt, much like an enema. My preference was smoking it, but I was not opposed to try different things. There are different ways meth can be smoked. I used a glass pipe, but when I could not get one, I used tinfoil. Debbie's suspicion really came about when she would find broken pieces of broken glass in the carpet. I would get so high that I would burn myself and drop the glass pipe, and it would break. I always thought I found all the pieces, but I never did. She would find the pieces of glass by stepping on them, and would ask me where these pieces of glass came from. I would always have an answer. The answer was never the truth, much like my answers for the shortages in my paycheck.

One day I was at my dealer's house, and I had told him that I needed a way to come with more money and I did not really care how I got it.

Fire and Faith

I started out doing small jobs like collecting debts from people who did not pay for what the drugs they were fronted. That did not last too long before my conscious caught up with me. There were some houses I would visit to get money from and there would be kids there. This was not a good scene. Sometimes there would be resistance from the guy who owed money and it would get physical. I remember the kids would be crying and cowering down to hide from the fight. However, I found another way to get a little free dope from time to time and that was by cleaning dope. This is a process where a person can get crappy meth and have the ability to clean it. The problem with this is that if you have a large amount of meth, when cleaned, you actually lose part of it. I am not going to go into the details of the cleaning process, but I can tell you that it is somewhat dangerous. I did this process for quite some time.

I remember one day a friend of mine was in his room at his apartment, while the rest of us were in the living room getting high. I had already been there for a long time and decided to go home. When I knocked at his bedroom door, I could hear him in there, and his torch burning. I knew that he was cleaning his meth. I told him I was taking off and that I would see him later. Later that evening, he was still cleaning and did not pay attention to what he was doing, and he set himself on fire. One of the stages of cleaning the meth is that the dope is in a Pyrex jar filled with acetone.

Acetone is very flammable. Then a lid is placed on it, and then heated to a boil. When it boils the flame is taken away to cool down. Then the flame is placed back under the jar and brought to a boil again. If you do not take the flame off at the moment of boil, the pressure builds and then it brakes. This is what happened to my friend. The jar exploded from the pressure and the acetone ignited, and well I am sure you can understand what happened from there. The jar contained about a half-gallon acetone which covered him and his bed. His room went into a blaze within seconds. When I heard what happened, I decided that I would not it anymore, no matter how much free dope I could get. Also there are other stages to cleaning meth, but for this book I wanted you to get the point.

Money was getting more and more difficult for me to get. I needed money for my habit, but the last thing I wanted to do was work for it, at least at a real job anyway. So I used my wife to get what I wanted. Whenever she would get paid I would take forty or fifty dollars at a time, and tell her she must have lost it, or miscalculated the money somehow. My other excuse was that I must have lost it. The only concern I had was my pipe. I wanted more and more meth, and I could not extinguish my craving no matter how much I had. The dealer that I used to get my drugs from was very liberal with her personal stash. I would go over every day and she would smoke about two hundred dollars' worth of dope with me and sometimes with the people that were there. However, you had to be part of the "click", and I was just that. This drug dealer was a heavy hitter in the drug world. Some of the information I cannot give out, because of the sensitivity to who was involved. So I will not give out any names at all. What I can tell you is that the dealings I did have during these times was much more than your local street pusher or drug dealer. I was close to the top at that time.

This particular dealer let's just say was connected very well. In fact she lived in an apartment complex on the bottom floor. I did a lot of "jobs" for her as I mentioned before. Anyhow, she lived on the bottom floor and all around her apartment were other apartments rented out for the watchers. The watchers were people that my dealer rented apartments for, for them to live in. There they would stay there and be fed dope to watch her apartment. They looked out for cops and other unwanted people. Their apartment had no furniture in it at all except a couple of lawn chairs and a mattress on the floor. Their job literally

Fire and Faith

was to watch, hence the name watchers. So with that being said, what happened next freaked me out.

My wife one day decided to leave work in the middle of the day and come find me. The amazing part was she did find me, which leads me to believe that someone snitched me out. Anyway she showed up at the door to this particular apartment, and it was not pretty. She was banging on the door screaming at the top of her lungs, "Joey I know you're in there!" When I got to the door she was screaming and yelling for me to leave and go home. All I kept thinking was she was making such a seen that I would have to suffer the consequences in some way shape or form. Meaning my family was now at risk. All through my drug days and dealings I have never allowed what followed drugs to come to my home. I led a double life. In fact one day I was working on a neighbor's car and a gentleman showed up there and he thought he knew me. He kept saying over and over again he knew me, right in front of my wife. Finally I leaned in real close and told him that if he said it again that I would kill him. He then stood back with a loud voice and said, "Oh my mistake I do not know you." Fortunately I after the whole situation with my wife coming to get me at the dealers house, I was able to make peace with certain people.

Fire and Faith

There would only be three people at my dealer's apartment at any given time. At the time what I thought was good, was I could smoke as much as I wanted to without having to pay for it. I was the kind of person who liked to get high with other people, but I always wanted to be able to go home with my own drugs. The truth is as much as I like to get high with other people, I also really liked getting high by myself even more. I loved to smoke it, just to see the smoke. I loved to get high alone knowing that I had drugs for the next day made my mood happy. There were times however, when I did not have money to buy meth and it would devastate me mentally.

Chapter 18

I did not always have money and I had to start getting creative in order to find money for my ever-increasing appetite for meth. Over the years, my wife and I had acquired a lot of things. So much stuff in fact that if something was to go missing it would not be noticed, especially things from my garage. I was able to take tools and things of that nature and pawn them off. I found this a quick way of getting a lot of money to feed my cravings. As my desire to get high grew, so did my desire to be away from home.

I was working nights at a grocery store at this time and normally get home about 7:30 a.m. I found myself getting home later and later. Debbie always thought once again that I was cheating on her. I mean think about it, I was spending money all the time and I could not account for it. I was never home and when I was, I was completely disconnected from her. My only joy for coming home at the time was for my daughter, who was still a baby at the time. This defiantly looks like I could be cheating in my book. I remember one morning I was at a friend's house and I got a phone call there. I freaked out. No one knew where I was, especially Debbie.

Fire and Faith

I answered the phone and her first question to me was, "What are you doing?" I knew I had been caught, but I did not know how she knew all the facts. She told me that I should probably come home so we could talk. I asked her why and she said "Just come home." I asked her why and she said "Jimmy told me what you've been doing." I went into a blind rage, and I headed home to tear Jimmy apart. How could he rat me out? I had been up for days and I was unable control my rage. I only knew that I had a loaded gun in my car, and that I was really, really pissed off at Jimmy.

One of the biggest problems I faced using meth for me was, when I was coming down, or "beyond tired" I would snap into a rage without warning. (Just to let the readers know now, I never snapped on my kids, and I thank God.) I drove recklessly on the way home and fortunately for Jimmy it was a long drive for me to get there. I pushed my Mustang 5.0 to the limits. The faster I drove the better I felt. I started to calm down a little on the way home, but not enough to face Jimmy. I figured if I got in the house I would shoot him. I decided to stop at another friend's house on my way home. I figured I would go there to calm down. I do not know why I thought to stop. I guess the Lord knew the outcome of what I would do. His name was Randy, and he did not do meth which was a good thing. I think if he did use meth I

Fire and Faith

would have gotten high there before going home. I told Randy what had happened, and he made sure I was calm enough to go home.

I left Randy's house and got back into my car burning rubber all the way down the road in my Mustang. As I rounded the corner to my street, I noticed I still had my loaded gun sitting in the console of my car. Driving as fast as I was down my street, I was lucky I did not hit someone. I drove my car right through the front yard up to front door. I remember looking in through the front window of the house and I saw Jimmy sitting on the couch. I also saw Debbie standing in the living room handing Jimmy a beer.

I got out of the car and bolted through the front door. I had my gun tucked underneath my arm. I had no intention of shooting Jimmy. I just thought I would scare him. What I did want to do though was beat him with my hands, but when I looked at him, I just could not bring myself to do it. I stayed mad enough though for him to think I was going to beat him up. He was so scared at the time, and I will never forget the look on his face. The both of them kept saying that they were worried that I had a problem. They also kept telling me that I needed to put my gun down as well. After about fifteen minutes, I started to calm down. I told Debbie that I had been doing meth and that I would stop. I promised them that I could quit. I was wrong. I still had a lot of meth in my pocket, and there was no way I was giving that up. I had no intention of truly quitting.

There was another part to meth that I fully enjoyed as well: sex. For some reason when a man uses a lot of meth, it has an effect on his libido. If my wife and I had sex it would go on for hours before I would climax. For me this was great, but for my wife it was borderline rape. For me it was all about feeding my sexual hunger, and when those needs were not met by my wife I found myself doing other things to occupy my time. I had to start doing something with my time. One of the things that took most of my time was going through the stuff in my garage and "organizing" it. On one night I would stay up all night long organizing everything we had, and then on the following night unpack everything and leave things a total mess. Another thing that soon got my attention was pornography. I would spend hours watching porno and that built up tension and then I would seek out my wife. My wife admitted to me recently that she love the spontaneity, but did not like who I was. She was basically sleeping with a stranger. I truly feel bad about what I did, and I have found forgiveness from her.

With all the sex that was going on, Debbie was pregnant again. (The amazing part was that I was always sober at the time of conception.) But I would be back into the drugs soon after. It was like

Fire and Faith

I would quit getting high for a couple of weeks, and then I would start back up again. I realize now that the only reason I quit was when I ran out of money, or I could not find my drug of choice; Most of the time it was because of money. I started getting bolder trying to find ways to get money, and one of those ways was to steal it. Instead of going out and stealing from other people though, I would steal from my wife. Stealing cash was one of the ways and was pretty easy to do and get away with. I always had some lie to back it up. The other way of stealing was the lowest of lows. My wife did not wear a lot of jewelry but she had a lot of it in her jewelry box. In fact one of the pieces she had was from my great aunt. It was an old ring with a lot of diamonds in it, and because she never would wear her jewelry it was easy to take.

I ended up pawning the ring for eighty dollars. The sad part to this was I stole the ring to begin with. The other part to this was that the ring was probably valued at 5000 dollars and I dumped it for 80 dollars. I sold a lot more jewelry, but the truth is I cannot remember just exactly what I sold anymore. In fact when I finally quit drugs for good, it became my mission to buy my wife jewelry on every occasion. My wife finally came to me and said that I was forgiven and I did not need to buy her anymore jewelry. I know that the reason I bought as much as I could was out of guilt for what I'd done. "It is horrible how guilt and shame can play in a person's life." The funny thing about forgiveness is that it is like a "do over card." Once I knew I was forgiven, not only did I stop buying so much jewelry, but what had been eating me up inside was finally laid to rest.

We decided to move across town to a bigger home for the new baby that was on the way. Another reason to move was to leave the neighborhood that was filled with my poison. Debbie was getting much bigger because of the pregnancy. She was getting close to delivering our next beautiful daughter. I was staying sober for the most part, and things seemed to be going ok. I had been sober for a couple of months working nights at the local grocery store. Before I knew it, I was in the delivery room awaiting my second daughter. She was born on August 3rd and was once again the most beautiful thing I had ever seen. A miracle takes place when a woman delivers a baby. She was so precious, and I could not wait to get her home. When I did finally get her home it seemed like trouble was waiting for me at my doorstep. I went back to work the following night to finish out the week. About the same time a new guy started at work, and for some reason I gravitated to him. He used meth, and I knew it. One Friday night I knew I did not have to go back to work until after the weekend. We worked together that night, and our conversation quickly made its way

Fire and Faith

to drugs. It just so happened that I had a large sum of money in my pocket, and I convinced him to sell me all that he had.

I basically locked myself in the bathroom the whole weekend and got high. Every time I turned around I was making my way back into the bathroom to get high. I knew that it would be easy to hide, since Debbie had just had the baby. I would sit on the toilet as if I was really going to the bathroom and set everything on the counter next to me. I would take a piece of toilet paper and get it wet. That way when my pipe got hot after each hit I could cool it by laying it on the wet paper. I saved a lot of dope that way and it lasted a lot longer. I would sit in there for about 15 minutes at a time and get high. The only problem I had to deal with was listening for Debbie walking by, because I did not want Debbie to hear the clicking sound of my lighter. At the time I used to smoke cigarettes, and I always lit one when I went in there. The problem was I would lay it on the counter and forget about it while I smoked my pipe. The counter tops were covered with cigarette burns.

When I was not in the bathroom, I was out in the front yard working on my Mustang. I was changing the oil and doing maintenance on the car. Earlier that week my car had been over heating, so I decided to check that issue as well. After I had finished the repair, I was letting the car idle to make sure it would not overheat again. While the car

244

Fire and Faith

was running I had my hand on the radiator to see if it was heating up. At some point while my oldest daughter (age three) was running around, she accidentally bumped into me. My hand slipped and went directly into the moving fan. My hand shot back at me and part of the knuckle on my middle finger flew apart. I quickly ran into the house and wrapped it with duct tape and told my wife that it would be ok. It is very obvious that this was the drugs talking and not me. I went on with my daily routine and went to work that night. After three days my finger was swollen with infection, but I continued to ignore it. Debbie would not quit bothering me about going to the doctor. When I first did it she told me to go to the doctor and get stitched up, but I refused. I was still getting high, and that was more important to me. It is amazing how a person on drugs will put the drugs first at all cost.

Two weeks passed, and my finger was the size of the bottom of a beer bottle. The rest of my hand was very swollen and I couldn't move the rest of my fingers. One morning after not sleeping for about three days, Debbie found me in the bathroom with a razor blade trying to slice my finger open. I remember looking up at her while I was sitting on the toilet seat, and I said "You need to take me to the doctor or I am going to die." We got the kids up and into the car and headed to the hospital. When we arrived at the emergency room they immediately

Fire and Faith

brought me in to look at my hand. I remember there were multiple doctors looking at my hand and asking why I had not come in sooner. I had no answer for them. They explained to me that if I'd waited another twenty four hours I would have been dead.

The infection was so bad that it had entered my bloodstream in and was causing irreparable damage to my hand and arm. They told me that they would probably have to amputate my arm at the shoulder. I told them that were not going to that, and they explained that the arm would have to at least come off at the elbow. I started to go into a rage and told them that I would kill them if I woke up to find any part of my arm gone. They instantly admitted me for emergency surgery, and opened the finger up for what they called an aggressive cleaning. I was not allowed to leave the hospital for seven days. The wound was left open for 5 days, and then they did another surgery to close the finger as best as they could. Most of the flesh had rotted off my finger so they were contemplating skin grafts.

The infection I had was a combination of infections; staph infection and streptococcus. But there was another strain of infection that the doctors had never seen before. Jokingly I asked the doctors to name the new infection after me. The problem was though that there was no room for joking. The only thing the doctors could do was throw every antibiotic at it, and hope that it worked. When I was discharged from the hospital, a nurse came by every date for a month to put intravenous antibiotics into a pick-line they'd inserted in my arm. Once we completed that round, there was another thirty days of oral antibiotics. It probably would have helped the doctors for me to tell them that I was on methamphetamines. I slept for most of the time that I was in the hospital due to the fact I was coming off of meth. When I returned home I stayed clean from drugs for the month that I needed the injections of antibiotics. Fortunately for me it worked. I did not have to have skin grafts and my finger healed up pretty good. I am still not able to bend the finger at the middle knuckle.

During that month I was stuck at home. I was sober, and that's when I really got close to the new baby and oldest daughter. I tried to do as much as I could with them, but it was not long before I wanted to be high again. I started looking for my old connections and started once again getting high. This time though it was going to be a whole lot different. We ended up moving just down the street because they were raising our rent on the new lease. This was completely my fault. I lost my job, and I was still spending money left and right for my drug habit. We moved into the new place, and I took a job at night again, stocking shelves. I fell into the trap with the new people I worked with

Fire and Faith

that shared my love for meth. My habit got larger and larger and I was

up to a two hundred dollar a week habit.

Chapter 19

Debbie and I got a phone call that my wife's mother was very ill. We left immediately to be with her mother and dad. After three days, and some hospital visits with no answers, we decided to go back home, so my oldest daughter could get back to school. As soon as we got home, Debbie's family called and said she needed to catch the next flight; her mother had taken a turn for the worse. I hate to say this, but I had no problem with Debbie flying out there. I knew that I would be able to get as high as wanted. Don't get me wrong, I felt horrible for Debbie and her mother, but the drugs (believe it or not), were more powerful than even that.

After Debbie flew out to be with her mother, I was supposed to drive the girls out to see their grandmother when Debbie said it was ok. So during this time I locked myself in my bedroom got high and watched pornography most of the time that she was gone. Every night Debbie called me to come to California and bring the kids out. I was so selfish and kept making excuses that I did not want the girls to see their grandmother like that. Just so I could stay home and be close to my drugs. How horrible I was during this time.

Fire and Faith

I had a friend of mine drop off probably the strongest meth I had ever done. I had been up for about three days and three nights, and Debbie called me and told me that I needed to leave right then. It was the night before Thanksgiving. She knew her mother was not going to make it another day. I think it was about eleven o'clock that night when I finally decided to drive out there. It was about an eight hour drive, and I was not doing well. I had a hard time staying awake as I drove the car. I remember looking into the back seat, and I saw my two precious daughters sleeping in their car seats while I struggled to stay awake. I had been on the road about five hours and I was starting to fall asleep. At one point I dozed off, and I felt someone grab my arm and give me a gentle shake. I woke up instantly and checked my girls. Both of them were sound asleep, and there was no one there to grab my arm.

We made it to the hospital early that morning only to find that no one from Debbie's family was there. Everyone had gone home, and I was standing in the hospital with my two daughters. I was hoping that they were not there, because I knew I looked horrible. My eyes were black and they looked as if they had sunk into my skull. I went to find a nurse and asked her where my wife's mother was. She led me down the hall, and then as we entered the room, the nurse realized that I

Fire and Faith

thought Debbie's mom was still alive. She looked at me and said that I was too late and she passed away just a couple hours before. Right then I knew who grabbed my arm in the car to wake me up. It was my wife's mother. I brought the girls to Debbie's parents' house where my wife was staying.

It was painfully obvious to my wife what I had been doing while she was gone. I let her down by not being there, and more importantly Debbie's mother for not getting her granddaughters to her in time. I was so ashamed showing up like I did. I was so high, and I know everyone knew it. I was a mess! The only thing I could do to avoid my wife's disappointment, was to pick a fight with her, so I could feel angry instead of ashamed. Everyone was looking at me, so I thought anyway. Most everyone would look at me and then look at my girls and shake their heads. To be truthful even after all of this, I just wanted to get high again just so I would not have to deal with the shame.

We had Thanksgiving dinner with her family all together, and after all arrangements were made, and conversations were over, two days later, we drove back home. The trip was horrible. My wife had just lost her mother, and I was a big disappointment to her. Once again, I thought and believed that I had blown it. Not just the marriage, and to be truthful, somewhere inside me I wanted Debbie to leave me. I wanted her to get on with her life and forget about me. My belief was that I was useless and worth nothing. See all my years of life I have always felt that way. When we got back home, we decided to move yet again.

We were moving up into a neighborhood that was even worse than the one we were in. This neighborhood looked much nicer than the one we came from, but it was the surrounding area that was bad. The area we moved to had a lot of drugs in it, and was pretty much the "meth hub" for all of Phoenix, Arizona. This is where drugs led me to a whole new dimension of hurting my family. Instead of just getting high, watching pornography, tearing things apart and putting them back together again, I found a better way to be high. I would start leaving in the middle of the night and go driving around town. This served two purposes. The first purpose (and most important) was that I would not be getting high in the house. The second purpose was that I felt completely free when I was gone. I did not have anyone to hide my shame from. The down side was that when I was home, I started using drugs in the house in a locked spare bedroom.

I completely neglected my daughters during the day while I was high. Once I was in bedroom getting high, the door would be locked for at least a couple of hours. During the day while my oldest daughter

Fire and Faith

was at school, I would be home with my youngest daughter. It was hell
for the both of them for me to be on drugs, but my youngest was the
one who did not see me until late afternoon. I remember being in my
chair in that spare bedroom and my youngest daughter would knock at
the door. This would start soon after she got bored with the cartoons I
made her watch in the morning. She would ask me if she could come
in and I would tell her no. I told her that daddy was busy and that I
would be out later. To a three year old that was forever. My daughters
just wanted to be with me, and play much like I'd wanted to be with my
dad at that age. She would knock and cry, pleading with me to come
out. I would tell her again, only with anger to stop bugging me. By the
time I realized how much time went by, I would open the door to find
her curled up in a ball on the floor sleeping. She would be there for
hours. Even now, I am having a hard time holding the tears back as I
write this.

Moving to this house started a whole new problem though. I started
hanging around some really bad people. Actually they were not bad
they just did a lot of bad things just like me. One of these people was a
guy that used to supply my drug habit. I did not know it, but he had
been stealing from me the whole time. He was stealing my guns, tools,
and whatever else he could find. One night I noticed that my hand gun

Fire and Faith

was gone, so Debbie and I called the police. It was kind of difficult having the police in my house while I was high, but I was able to pull it off without being caught.

The police showed up to the house and we gave a report to what was stolen, and we were told that they would send a detective out that week. I had no idea that the detective was going to sit outside the home and watch me for a few days to see if I was behind the robberies. The detectives finally showed up at my house and they started asking me all kinds of questions. I thank God my wife was not there. Debbie was at work during this time and my oldest daughter was at school. The detective was implying that I sold all of the stuff that was reported stolen. I became completely pissed off them. The detective told me that they were going to go and question my five year old daughter at school to find out if I stole the guns. That's when I hit the roof. I was so angry at the police for going to the school and putting my daughter through that questioning.

Before they left my house there was a knock at the front door. When I opened the door, one of my drug dealers was standing there and telling me to let her in. I told her that this was not a good time and right then the detective said "No. Let her in." I looked at the detective and said "No.", but they were insistent, that she come in. They started asking her all kinds of questions about the things that were stolen. I quickly interrupted the questioning and told them that they needed to leave. The detectives called my wife that day and told her that another woman showed up to the house, which caused Debbie to question me that night when she came home. I could never tell Debbie that I had a friend that was female, let alone that she was my drug dealer.

Debbie and I fought that night into the late hours of the night. I remember that the fight was getting pretty intense and I was on the verge of doing something that I had never done before. I was ready to hit her. Right at the moment as I was ready to swing at her, my daughter walked into the kitchen with a sword that I had in my room, and she stabbed into the floor and screamed "Stop fighting!" Believe it or not, that was just enough to stop me from doing something I would have regretted for the rest of my life. I have done a lot of things in life that I have regretted, but that is the wonderful thing about forgiveness. [I will talk more about that later.] We went to bed that night angry with each other. I should say that Debbie went to bed. I stayed up for the rest of the night as usual. I always had a problem with accusations. I understand that I did a lot of things wrong, but if was accused for something I did not do, I would get really upset.

Fire and Faith

The next morning, Debbie went to work and I got my oldest

daughter off to school and I waited for my other drug dealer. This guy

was not only my dealer, but I thought he was a friend as well. I was

wrong. He showed up about nine o'clock in the morning. I knew that

he was bringing me some meth so I could get high, and I was ready

after the night I just had with Debbie. He walked in the house with a

case that held his music cd's. When he opened it he had a big bag of

meth in there and that is what we were going to smoke. I told my

littlest daughter to go outside and play, because daddy needed to talk

privately to his friend.

He pulled the bag of meth out of the case, and set the case on the

floor next to the chair he was sitting in. During this time I was so

focused on the bag of meth, I was not paying attention to my daughter.

She grabbed that case my friend had and opened it up. Before I knew it

she had pulled all of the cd's out along with a bunch of yellow papers.

When I looked down she had already made a mess and so I yelled at

her for the mess she made. As I got to the floor to pick up the mess, I

realized that the yellow pieces of paper were actually receipts from the

pawn shop. As I started to look a little more closely I noticed that the

first line on receipt said Ruger 45. That was my gun! I looked at him

Fire and Faith

and then looked at my daughter. I told my daughter to go outside and not to come back in until I came to get her.

She walked away slowly, and I heard the sliding glass door open and then shut. I looked back at my so-called friend and proceeded to beat the hell out of him. I beat him from the living room all the way into the kitchen. As he was trying to crawl away, I looked up and saw my daughter looking through the sliding glass door. I immediately stopped, and dragged him out the front door. I wrote down his license plate number and called the police. The police did absolutely nothing about it. I had only about an hour before Debbie got home and I had to clean up the blood before she got home. Unfortunately my daughter had seen everything; a memory that I cannot erase from her.

I tried to get the floor cleaned up and I was pretty successful. The down side to that was my three-year old daughter love to tell the events of each day to my wife when she came home from work. And that is exactly what she did. I remember I was in the living room watching television, when my wife walked in asking how my day went. She asked me if there was anything I needed to tell her. I told her that the day was normal, except that I had found out who had stolen all of our stuff. I also told her that I called the police to turn him in. Now my biggest concern was not for what my daughter had witnessed, and it

Fire and Faith

was not the stuff that had been stolen from the house. My biggest

concern now was where I was going to get the drugs that I needed.

I always made it a habit in every location we lived, to always keep

tabs on the neighbors. I was always on the lookout for people up until

two-o'clock in the morning working on their car, or up all night for no

reason. If I found those people, that would mean I found my drugs.

Most people that stayed up all night long like me were usually using

some kind of drugs. I always looked for the guy that was really skinny,

always sweating for no reason, and the one you never saw eating. If I

saw this guy I knew I could find the drug of my choice. There was a

house just two doors down from my own that I was going to take a

chance on. I will never forget this because people just don't do this

type of thing unless they are desperate. I went into the room that I used

to get high in and grabbed my glass pipe and what little bit of meth I

had. I poured the rest of my meth into the pipe and walked over to the

neighbor's house.

I knocked at the door and when the man opened the door, I held my

pipe up and asked him if he could help me out. He looked at me like I

was out of my mind and he probably thought that I was a cop. I put the

pipe to my mouth and lit it up and smoke a bowl right in front of him.

He grabbed me, pulled me inside and said "Ok you made your point,

Fire and Faith

you're not a cop!" I handed him eighty dollars and told him to go get

me a big bag of meth. He told me that eighty dollars would get me an

"eight ball"... I thought this was wonderful! An eight ball usually cost

me about one-hundred forty dollars, and now I was getting a lot more

for a lot less. An eight ball refers to how much meth is in the bag, and

my habit at the time was about two eight-balls a week. He told me to

go back to my house and wait for him to return. He came back within a

few minutes with the best meth I had ever had. I smoked so much that

day, and I had never been that high. It was unbelievable! I knew I

wanted more and more.

Chapter 20

When my wife returned home that night from work, I was looking for anything to argue about, just so I could leave. I did not have the guts to just get up and leave, which probably would have been better. But what I did do was dig for a fight, and I would totally blow it out of proportion. I was so nasty to her. I would call her every name in the book, and completely belittle her to the point of tears. "To be truthful I believe that I actually hated her for not leaving me. I was so mad that she would allow "me" to be a dangerous stranger in the home. I did not care to be a husband, and I did not care to even be anything in that home. I wanted to go and hang out with friends, and get high all night long. When I could not find anyone around I would hang out at the local parks late at night when no one was there, and get high all night long by myself. In the beginning I would not travel far so I could be close to the house. I was always worried that someone may try to break into my house while I was away. I believe the drugs not only got me really high, but it brought on a lot of paranoia. During these nights most of the time, I would leave on my bike.

I would be out from about ten-o'clock at night until about four or five-o'clock in the morning. I would sneak out the front door and then

Fire and Faith

sneak in like a thief in my own house. Then the rest of my day consisted of me finding and doing as much drugs I could possibly do. To be perfectly honest I am not sure why I tried to do as much as I could. "I honestly believe that I was trying to kill myself secretly. Meaning, I did not have the guts to shoot myself, so I was basically doing a slow kill to myself." I knew at times if I took one hit off the pipe I would probably die, but it did not stop me. I had friends that were overdosing on a lot less than what I was doing. It seemed like there was no limit as to how much I could do. Because of that thinking I kept pushing the envelope.

By this point my own mother was telling Debbie to leave me. I mean seriously, could anyone blame her? I was out of control and had been for five years. Everyone knew that I was on a path of destruction. Everyone in Debbie's family was saying the same thing, divorce him and leave. My wife is an incredible woman. During this whole time of destruction she never gave me the thought that she would leave me. Divorce was never an option for her. My wife had to not only deal with me through this journey, but she also had to deal with everyone around her telling her to just leave me. My wife knew that I was in trouble, and she always did her best to be there in my time of need. I sometimes wonder how my wife and children could offer so much forgiveness. I also fully believe that God can perform any miracle for any person in any circumstance. I also fully believe that, I have learned more about the gospel through my wife and children. I see and feel firsthand what true forgiveness is through them. By saying that I was forgiven, I was able to learn how to truly forgive myself.

Unfortunately my story does not end here. By this time I was stealing from everyone and selling everything to get my drugs. I was not even close to hitting the bottom yet. I was just getting started! During this time, my wife received another phone call from her family informing her that her father was not doing well. My wife came to me, and fortunately I was about three days sober, and she told me that she wanted to move to California to be closer to her dad. At first I was pissed off to think that I had to be away from my addiction. I thought to myself, what am I going to do now? Never mind the fact that my wife had already lost her mother and now was probably going to lose her father. I was so selfish. Everything was about me and my addiction. The only thing I kept thinking was that my wife was going to leave regardless of my answer, and I needed to figure out a way to get enough drugs to take with me. Sounds pretty stupid huh?

We had about two weeks before we were going to move and I was on the hunt to start gathering as much dope as I could possibly get. I

Fire and Faith

was still leaving at night pulling the same crap as usual with my wife. I would leave in the middle of the night, and return home in the morning. Except one night I left on my bike and decided to ride around through the parks at night, which happened to be one of my favorite things to do while I was high. On this night though I had been up for a couple of days and I was already starting to hallucinate from the lack of sleep. Hallucinating was common for me, if I had no sleep for an extended period of time. I always saw "shadow people", especially at night. From a distance it always looked like someone was walking around, but by the time I got there, then there would be no one there. I was riding my bike on the sidewalk and returning home, when a truck pulled out in front of me and I slammed into the truck. The only thing I remember was seeing the taillights of the truck leaving. My bike was destroyed and I had a long walk home.

I called my wife at a payphone and she agreed to come and get me. Even after leaving and getting high, she still came to get me and make sure I was ok. I still did not learn anything from that experience and I was back out that night in the car this time. I was trying to line up deals so I could at least put together about an ounce of dope to take with me to California. There was only one problem to trying to save up all my meth. I couldn't stop myself from smoking whatever I got, so

Fire and Faith

there was no way of saving any of it. The first week passed very quickly. We would be moving in just a few days. My wife had the whole house packed and was ready to leave as soon as possible. During this time, I was no help whatsoever, and I was really starting to be a real jerk because I knew my time was short. I think in a way I wanted her to move on without me, in fact I know I wanted her to. I was constantly smoking my meth and getting absolutely no sleep and did not care about anything but that. Not to mention I was now eating meth as well.

We got the truck two days before we had to leave so we had the whole day to pack it and then leave the following morning. I still had not had any sleep at all and I had been up for a total of four days. I was waiting for a friend of mine to show up because I really needed to get high. I could barely stay awake and I need to help pack the truck. My wife was home, and there was no way I was going to be able to get and pay for the dope while she was at home. I told her that she needed to run to the store to get something to drink for me. I figure that would be enough time for my friend to slip in and out before she got back. When I asked her to go she said she had too much to do and that if I wanted something to drink, I should go and get it. I agreed so I got into the car and drove to the local convenience store and waited for my friend there.

Fire and Faith

When I got to the store he was right behind me, and we quickly made the exchange. I was so relieved that I at least had enough dope to get me high and still had a little for the trip. As soon as my friend left the parking lot, I decided to sit right there in my car and take a few hits, before going in the store getting my drink. The last thing I remember was that I took my pipe out of my pocket and placed it on one side of my lap, and I placed the bag of dope on the other side of my lap. I must have put my head back for a second, and before I knew it, I was out like a light. I must have fallen asleep pretty hard because I was parked right in front of the store with everything in my lap for six hours. I am sure many people saw me there sleeping. I was lucky that no one called the cops. I would have been arrested for sure. I used to sometimes think to myself that I would have been better off being arrested instead of putting my family through the hell that I put them through. Just as important as my family, I put myself through hell as well.

(The effects of the meth had been taking a serious toll on my body for a long time and they were only getting worse. My finger was already destroyed from the infections that I had, and was in the hospital for. My fingers and hands would crack and bleed. My feet were just as bad. My toenails were yellow and thick from the bacteria that lived

Fire and Faith

under them. The cracks in my fingers were terrible pain for me, and yet that was still not enough for me to quit. As soon as I would make a fist in the morning, the sides of my fingers would split wide open. I would soak my hands in lotion and where socks on my hands and feet to help heal them.

Sometimes the splits on my fingers and feet were so bad, that I could see all of the meat inside right down to the bone. Then they would get massively infected, which required me to make a doctor visit and take antibiotics. I was very dehydrated from the meth, because I did not drink any water, or anything for that matter. My skin always had a grey hue to it, and always had dark circles under my eyes. I also have permanent vision damage, because my eyes were always dilated and I never protected my eyes.) I had severe headaches, that were bad enough for me to puke and sometimes I would put my head between the mattress and box spring of my bed. The pressure from the weight of the bed sometimes relieved the pain. This would happen more than a couple times a week.

(I would also find myself bleeding just after a bowel movement. There was no pain, but when I would wipe with toilet paper it would be covered in blood, and then it would stop. I remember the first the first time that had happened and I thought I was dying. Someone once said

Fire and Faith

"That is the way the body purges itself." (I'm not sure if that is true or not.) All I do know is that it happened so many times that I was used to seeing this at least a couple of times a week. Most of my teeth (ninety-eight percent) were rotting. I had horrible toothaches most of the time because of the infections. I remember the back ones would break just from eating something as soft as a piece of cheese. As long as they were the back ones, no one could see the damage from the use of meth.

The front were rotting as well, but it was at the top of the teeth, so I just would not smile as or as big. The top of my teeth, near the gums was black from rot. Since my meth use I went in for surgery and had 29 extractions done at one time. They put in 135 stitches to sew my gums back up, and I now have dentures. "They are pretty dentures, but nevertheless dentures." When my teeth were removed, it was the best thing for me, but there was tremendous loss to me. It was like losing an arm or a leg. Meaning, I never realized what it was like to have to use something fake. My lungs had been affected by the meth use as well. I would have at least one bronchial infection every three months. I would have fluid in my lungs, which required me to go to emergency to get breathing treatments and inhalers just so I could breathe somewhat normally, but even that did not stop me from doing meth. I was going downhill fast.

Fire and Faith

After I woke up in the car, I had no idea what time it was. It was still day light but the sun was setting quick. I realized I had been there for hours sleeping. I quickly started the car and made my way back to the house. I was in such a panic to hurry and get home that I dropped my pipe along the side of the seat. I pulled over to the side of the road and got out of the car. I reached in to tilt the seat forward and when I did, the seat cable broke, locking the seat in the forward position. Now I could not get back into the car and drive because the seat was stuck forward. I remember, that I was thinking that Debbie would never believe what had happened with the seat.

By the time I got home, Debbie was extremely mad at me because I had been gone the whole day. When she asked where I was, I came up with a lie and quickly made my way to the floor in the living room to get more sleep. I was so tired and rundown that I literally could not stay awake. The only thing I knew was that I had to drive the moving truck soon, so I needed as much sleep as I could get, just so I could make the seven-hour drive. I was hallucinating that their where wild animals in the house. I could see elephants and monkeys. Then I thought I saw a truck with a trailer coming through the living room. There was every walk of wild life on this truck. There monkeys

Fire and Faith

driving the truck, and I even yelled out to Debbie asking her if she was
looking at what was going on

Chapter 21

The next morning came quickly and it was time to leave for California. While I was driving the moving truck, my wife drove our two daughters in our car. It was a seven-hour drive and I had nothing but time on my hands, so I did some thinking along the way. I decided rather than try and find new drug dealers I would try and get sober. I figured the best way to get sober was to not have anyone you know doing drugs. After coming to this conclusion, I reached into my pockets and grabbed my pipe and my bag of meth, and threw it out the window on the freeway. I told myself that I was done with it, and I would not return to it. We had a few serious issues getting to California. The truck caught on fire, and had to be towed one-hundred miles, and no money for a motel when we arrived because the plans that were made with my step-sister hadn't been relayed to her husband, and she was out of state.

Still, I felt really good about my decision to leave meth behind me. What I did not realize or plan on was the mood problem I was going to have. In the past when I came off of meth, I would just sleep for days until I was able to handle staying awake. This time was different though. I did not get to sleep it off and that made me very dangerous.

Fire and Faith

When we went to the hotel for the night they had no more rooms. So went to the only other hotel that the town offered.

I remember there was an Asian man there and he was not very friendly, and he was not budging on the price of the hotel. The room was 49 dollars according to the sign and that is exactly what I had. He would have no part of it though, because I did not have enough for tax. I told him that I had two children in the car and reminded him that it was 1am in the morning. I even told him we would leave at 6am, and that I just needed to let my daughters sleep a few hours. He still refused! That's when I lost all control and I started yelling racial slurs and obscenities and then I proceeded to smash the glass window. I remember hearing Debbie yelling at me to get in the car. She kept thinking that I was going to be arrested. We left the hotel and returned about 45 minutes later and Debbie was able to get the room. For some reason he did not see her, because I was such a jerk, and his attention was only on me.

The next morning, we left the motel, and returned to Karla's to get settled and put our things in storage. But when we arrived, my brother-in-law told us that Debbie needed to call her sister right away. Debbie's father had had a stroke, and was in the hospital and it did not look good. He had just lost his wife nine months prior, and now it looked as

Fire and Faith

if he was going die soon himself. Debbie's parents were the same age as my grandparents and Debbie was born when her parents were in their forties. All of Debbie's sisters and brothers are my parent's age. One of my biggest problems is being sensitive to my wife's needs. For some reason I am not equipped to show sensitivity when she is going through a difficult time. I become overwhelmed with the feeling of guilt and shame. When I feel that much guilt and shame it was easier for me to be medicated than it was for me to face the problem and work through it. Soon after we received the news that Debbie's dad had a stroke we drove to the hospital to see him.

When we arrived at the hospital he laid in the bed motionless. The doctors told us that he could hear us but he was not able to talk. Debbie's whole family was there and they went in one by one to visit him. I was one of the last to make it in to see him. Before I went into his room, I went to the gift shop and bought a little silver angel that had the word "courage" engraved in it. By the time I came back everyone had already been in to him. I told Debbie that I wanted to see him before we left, so I walked in and sat down on the bed. I picked up his hand, and placed the angel in it. While placing it in his hand I told him out loud that I promised I would take care of his daughter. I told him that he did not have to worry about her, and that I would always be

Fire and Faith

there for her. For some reason I felt that I needed to tell him this, after all Debbie was the baby of the family.

We left that afternoon only to return to my stepsister's chaotic house. I had full intention to fulfill my promise to that man, but as you will see later that did not happen. It is not that I did not have the heart to do so. The problem I was facing was my addiction and that seemed so much stronger than anything in my life. I really wanted to be a better man. I really wanted to be a better husband and father. But the addiction grew stronger the longer I denied it. Five days later, I told Debbie that I needed to handle some issues back in Arizona, and that I would be back the next day.

The last time my mother and I spoke was not a great situation. My mother had given Debbie money to leave me. Also our conversation was not the best when we had left. So by telling Debbie that I needed to go to Arizona to resolve the issues was somewhat true. However, I had a hidden agenda. I planned on running into some old friends for a hook up. I told Debbie that I would just do a turnaround trip and that I would be back by the next day.

The whole drive through the desert on my way back Arizona was nothing short of excitement. I knew that when I got there I would find my way back to a bag of dope. I knew that my friends would ready to

Fire and Faith

party. I figured I would have to come up with quick cash so I was prepared to sell my guitar and anything else of value that I could stuff in my car. Debbie had no idea of the things I put in the car to sell. I had a couple of car stereos that were stolen. I had amps, speakers, cds, and other miscellaneous items that had some value. My intention was to bring back about two 8balls (quarter ounce) of meth. When I did arrive there, I did get dope, but I did just about all of it while I was there. Before I knew it I was sitting back in South Phoenix at a drug den, with so many people I did not know. My time went by quickly and I knew I needed to head back to California. My wife had no mode of transportation, considering I had the only car. It took me close to four days to return, and Debbie's dad passed away two days later.

I spent the next few days cleaning up again, only to try to quit for good. However, staying with Karla was a disaster. I was trying to get sober in a place where everyone was using some type of drugs. In fact the only ones who were not using meth or drugs were my wife and I, oh and of course the children. I knew it was only a matter of time before I would start using, and so did my wife. For a few weeks I managed to handle not using meth. But the addiction haunted me and came to visit me once again. Sadly, people who use drugs always seem to find a way into my life or should I say, I find my way into theirs. After three long weeks, my wife got in contact with her sister and her husband and they agreed that we could stay there at their house.

We stayed at their house for one year. That was a long year. We moved into their three bedrooms home and we basically lived on an air mattress in their living room for the first three months. During this time we were to look for jobs and save money to get our own place. No one had any idea of my addiction and they just thought I was troubled person who could not get his life straight. It was not long though before my true colors started to show. Debbie was able to secure a job very quickly. She has always been very marketable and can do anything. Her new position brought really good money, but my skills were limited. I have always been able to fix or build anything, but for some reason I could not find employment. My wife has a niece whose husband had and operated his own business. He was nice enough to bring me on with his crew and help do lighting for client's homes. It was not long before the conversation at work got onto drugs. There were two guys that worked for him that secretly got high and the owner or Debbie's "nephew" did not know. Before you know it, I was picking them up and we were riding together to work and getting high with meth.

Fire and Faith

Once again I was getting up in the middle of the night and leaving to go driving around and get high. Every chance I got to smoke meth I would. I had a hard time hiding my paraphernalia from my wife and her family. I had to get creative. In Arizona I kept most everything on me but when I did sleep, I would usually have to find a hiding place for my meth. Debbie found my pipes and bags of meth from time to time, and I would always awake to her standing there asking me "Where did this come from?" I immediately started thinking of a lie and denied that it was ever mine. I would give her excuses and say that it was a friends', or that I had found it. It was always a lie and sounded much like a child's lies.

And then a new evil started up in me again: porno houses. These places sold pornography video tapes and they had video rooms inside. A person could go inside a room and watch pornography videos for a small fee. I would visit these places when I was up for a few days, and I could not find satisfaction at home. (After careful research I found that I had a sexual dysfunction due to the rapes in my early years). I was also supercharged on meth, and my sexual appetite was beyond control. Being very realistic though, there was no way I could blame my wife for not wanting to be with me.

Fire and Faith

The truth is that she wanted to be with me, but she did not want to be with person I had become. But, when I was high on meth my sexual thirst could not be easily quenched. So I seemed to pull away from my wife more and more every day. The porno houses were a place for release. These places are filled with homosexuals looking to please anyone orally, and they also had prostitutes that would do the same. Some of these places have private rooms and some of these rooms are private enough for two. Also the use of meth within the gay community is out of control. (Straight men are finding their way into the gay communities because of the use of meth. The same is true for women, but this subject is for my next book.)

I continued to work with Debbie's nephew and it was not long before I made up an excuse why I could not work for him anymore. I used to tell Debbie that I was looking for work during the day and of course that was a lie as well. I could usually be found at the apartment of my old co-workers getting high. They lived in a two bedroom drug den. There were always people there getting high. There were using heroine, meth, cocaine, weed, and on occasion, alcohol.

There were always girls there just waiting to get high. In fact my dealer used to say "The man with the bag has the power." Meaning if you had the bag of drugs or dope you could ask anything from the girls.

Fire and Faith

Don't get me wrong, there were plenty of days and nights where I wanted to take advantage of this so-called power. The truth of it however, was that I was always a little nervous to do so. If anyone is thinking that I did not take advantage of this because I was faithful, they are wrong. I was not even faithful to myself. All of my cares and morals were pretty much out the window. I believe the real concern was catching some type of sexually transmitted disease (STD). The last thing I wanted to add to the pot of destruction was a disease that could be transferred to my wife.

Chapter 22

"Death Awaits"

For the next couple of months I continued to hang out at this apartment. I would be there for a couple of days and then return back home to my wife sister's house, and sober up for a couple of days. Then once I could get enough money up, I would return back to the apartment and buy more drugs and start the cycle all over again. The only way I could leave the house feeling justified in my actions was that I would pick a fight with my wife. I would escalate the fight to a point that I would not feel guilty for leaving, at least for that moment. The guilt would always come back ten-fold once I sobered up. But, I would start another fight, so I could leave and start the cycle all over again. My guilt was something I could not live with sober. I knew I was destroying the lives of my children, my wife, and most importantly myself. I used to say "I would die for my kids and wife." A close friend of mine later corrected me in saying that I should live for them instead. That beautiful saying would not stick with me for about another year or so.

Fire and Faith

My wife worked for a place during this time and made really good money. This was my main source of money for my destruction. In the beginning, I would lie and hide the small amounts of money I took. Then, slowly I began taking larger amounts of money and did not even take the time to lie. I would just simply take it. During this time, everyone around my wife was telling her "Divorce him. Kick him out," everyone except for my wife's sister who we were living with. My wife's sister kept telling my wife that God had a different plan for me, and that I would be delivered in His time. Everyone thought she was crazy, including me! As I mentioned earlier my wife made good money, and one particular day I made plans to take it all. I don't think I planned it consciously, but that is what happened.

I woke up after sleeping for a few days and it was late afternoon. When I got up, my wife was ready to have a conversation about my disappearing at night and not coming home for days at a time. Our conversation went from zero to one-hundred in a matter of minutes. We were yelling at the top of our lungs at each other. The fight was so bad that my two daughters at the time went into the living room away from us and sat with my wife's sister. Our fight continued for several minutes as we soon made our way from the bedroom into the kitchen. I remember yelling so loudly that I was losing my voice, and it was

Fire and Faith

difficult to catch my own breath. As I walked out of the kitchen trying to make my way to the front door, I looked over my shoulder and saw my two daughters standing next to my wife's sister. They were crying and scared of the monster that they had just seen in me.

That screaming monster stopped for a brief moment, and I turned to them and said "I am sorry. I love you." At that moment my wife's sister said very calmly "You don't love them." When I heard those words leak from her lips, I turned towards her and got right in her face and said "How dare you, you fat @ss! Who do you think you are?" I wanted to hit her! I was in a rage that I almost could not control. At that moment the front door slammed shut and I looked behind me to see that her husband had come to her rescue. I quickly spun around and got right in his face, I said in a challenging loud voice "What are you going to do old man?" In a quiet and loving voice he responded, "I love you." I did not know what to do with that. I was so awe- struck by what he just said to me, that I had to leave. I looked at my wife and demanded the bank card and told her I would be back in the morning.

My wife followed me out the front door to the car. She told me that we were going to leave the following morning and go back to Arizona, but for some reason I did not believe her and I decided to go and get some money from the ATM. I went to the nearest store and pulled the maximum amount out. I believed that she was going to shut off the card before I could get money out so I went to get as much as I could before she did. Then just after midnight I was able to take out the maximum amount again. Over the next ten days, I was able to get a total of over four-thousand dollars. With this amount of money, I was able to have the party of a lifetime. I was able to buy more meth than I had ever had at one time, and it was going to be the death of me.

After collecting all of the money, I went back to the drug apartment and immediately had the dealer bring me a huge amount of dope. At this point, my memory gets very fuzzy and I only remember bits and pieces. From what I remember, the dealer showed up and I began to hand him a lot of money, not all of it, but a lot of it. I remember sitting at the table and there was about three or four of us smoking as much as we could. I remember shortly thereafter we went to the bedroom where we continued to smoke. There was about nine or ten people in the room and we were non-stop in this smoking and snorting frenzy. The minutes quickly turned to hours and hours into days. I had never been that high before. The only way I can describe it was that my body became a shell and I dwelled inside. I had no control of my actions. It was almost as if I was split into two people and my eyes were tiny windows to watch what was happening. I had no say in what my body was doing.

I remember that at one point, I heard someone say that we going to play a trick on one of the girls there, and tell her that the meth we were smoking was from outer space. She was a gullible girl, but we wanted to see how far we could take it. At this point though, I was unable to separate reality from fiction. (I am not sure of all the details, but I am trying my best to remember all of it.) As the night progressed, I became a totally different person than myself. It was almost as if a split personality came about. I was able to see what I was doing, but completely unable to control anything I was doing. I became someone I'd never met before; a personality that was nothing like mine. (This experience has never happened again since that time, and as far as I know, there was no permanent damage done.) I had been up for at least five days with no food or drink except for an occasional beer, in additional to all the chemicals in my body from the methamphetamine. I had probably smoked and snorted well over a half ounce which is completely unheard of in such a short period of time.

After going on for a while about this so called "space dope," I somehow managed to get on laughing kick. It was scary and almost seemed as if my brain was on a skip mode like a record or cd that had a

Fire and Faith

scratch in it. I kept repeating the same laugh over, and over again for what seemed like hours. I don't know where the strength came from but I was able to control myself for a brief minute. At that point, I was able to get up and get out of the room and make my way to the hallway that led to another bedroom. When I exited the room I looked to the left and saw a man standing there leaning against the wall. He was not really there when I reached towards him, but nonetheless, I saw a man standing there. This man was looking at me with great disappointment, and the only thing I could do at the moment was stare at him. I turned and went into one of the other bedrooms which were where one of the girls stayed in with her mother. Both the mother and daughter there were drug users. The daughter was about ten years younger than me and the mother was about eight years older than me. If I am not mistaken there were five people that lived in the apartment. But there were usually ten to fifteen people there at any given time.

As I made my way to the bedroom I found no one in it. I thought to myself, "If I lay down for a while I would somehow bounce back to normal." (Meaning my brain would go back to normal.) I remember looking around the room. There were two twin beds in the room. One on one wall and the other was on the other side of the room. On the third wall there was a dresser with a large mirror. As walked into the

Fire and Faith

room I remember leaning against the dresser with my back to the mirror. It only felt like a few seconds and suddenly there were two girls standing in front of me.

The first girl seemed very familiar to me. I could not see her face for some reason, but I knew who she was somehow. Her name was Linda. The second girl was the girlfriend of the guy who rented the apartment, and her name was Sherry. She was a little strange, and I knew for some reason that she liked me. This girl always seemed to be wherever I was, and always wanted to have sex with me. She made it very obvious what she wanted and said to me, "No one will find out. Come on!" To be perfectly honest there were times when I was high; I had a hard time controlling my sexual desires. The truth is I did not do anything with her, as far as I know.

As I mentioned before, I was able to see what was happening around me, but I was unable to control myself. My words and physical movement were out of my control. It was almost as if I was one inch tall trapped in my six-foot, one-inch body. Like a mere spec looking out of a body that was not my own, and completely at the will of whatever that body wanted to do. I can only imagine what a person with schizophrenia would go through. Maybe even like my souls was detached from my body somehow. What I do know is that anything

Fire and Faith

could have happened during those days and I would not have been able

to control it. The only way I can describe it, is if the soul would have

not part of the flesh and it literally separated itself from my body.

I remember that I told Sherry some really strange story that I had

just flown in from some other city, and I was at their apartment to buy

drugs and have sex with as many girls as possible. The truth is I could

not control the words coming out of my mouth, nor could I control my

actions. As the words were coming out it was as if someone else was

talking for me. Right at that moment I un-buttoned my pants and slid

them down. I remember that Sherry was smiling and looking towards

Linda as if she was waiting on a "Yes" answer from her. Sherry was

very excited to engage in a three way relationship. The other girl Linda

was standing to my left and she grabbed my pants and pulled them back

up and buttoned back up. I remember very little except that she laid me

down on the floor, and put my head in her lap for me to rest.

At this point I was completely out of my mind and I had a hard time

staying conscious. I thought it was about 2 in the afternoon at this

time, but every time I would gain consciousness it would be dark. I

had no sense of time or direction or anything about myself. I was lost

in my own confusion. I remember Linda left me alone while I was

lying down on the floor. During this time people were coming in and out of the room. I had such a hard time staying conscious, and I was not sure who was even in the room, but I remember hearing the door open from time to time.

While this was going on, I guess people thought it was the appropriate time to steal from me. They took all my drugs and cash. I was left with nothing. I should have been in the hospital at this time for a massive drug overdose, but no one cared. The only one there that seemed to care at all was Linda. During brief moments of consciousness, I remember lying on Linda's knees while she wiped the sweat off my face. I was sweating heavily, and could not move my body. I felt nothing from the neck down and my vision was dark at best. I could only see about 2 feet in front of me, and everything beyond that was shadows and blurs. I remember Linda kept asking me if I was ok and I could not respond. (Keep in mind that I had smoked and ate about 3 eight balls in the last 26 hours, and not to mention however much I did during the four or five days prior.) At one point she got up and brought several people in the room and I remember one guy saying he just needs something to eat.

I had not eaten or had any water in six or seven days. Someone said, "Just go get him a cheeseburger and he will be fine." The truth is I was not fine. I guess Linda got pretty scared because she tried to

Fire and Faith

wake me because I had stopped breathing for long periods of time.

One of the times she woke me, I happened to hear someone pounding

on the front door. I looked up at Linda and I said "That is my mother."

There was no way it was my mother though. At the time she was four-

hundred miles away and no one knew where I was. Suddenly,

everything went completely silent and black. It only seemed like a

moment, and then I was waking up to Linda's mouth pressed against

mine, and her hands were beating my chest. I was awake enough to ask

her what she was doing and she replied that I had died.

What I did not know was at the time, on that night, my oldest

daughter wrote a note to God. The note said "Dear Jesus, Please touch

my Daddy's heart and bring him home." Just as I heard Linda say that

I died, it went silent again and then to complete darkness. What

seemed like a blink of an eye was actually more than two minutes that

my heart had stopped. Linda was able to bring me back, and this time I

actually stayed alive. When I woke, my clothes were soaking wet from

sweat and I was really cold. Now I have to tell you that I did not see

any bright lights as described from people with a near death situation.

What I saw was black and cold. No sounds, smells, or taste. For lack

of a better description, there was nothingness.

Fire and Faith

After being awake for several minutes I could actually smell cheeseburgers. Someone actually went and got me a cheeseburger. They got the burger with the money they had stolen from me, but at least they got me one. I was able to sit up just long enough to eat the burger, and then I went back to sleep. I slept there on the floor for the next two days or so. To be truthful I did not realize how many days actually past. From the time I started partying to the day I finally left there was a total of seventeen days away from my wife and kids. To this day when I think about it, it only seemed like four days at the most that I was gone. When I did wake up, it was because Linda was telling me that I had to leave and it was an emergency. My wife had been trying to call my cell phone to tell me that my oldest daughter was hurt. In the message I could hear my daughters in the background saying "We love you daddy, please come home." My wife was trying to tell me that they had to take my daughter to the hospital. I laid there on the floor because I simply did not have the strength to get up. I was too weak from no food, drink and all the methamphetamine in my system.

I knew that I needed to get home to my children. I hate to say this, but I knew that my daughter was hurt, and that made me get up. I also need to be very honest as well. The longer I stayed away from the family the easier it got. The drug is all consuming and it destroys

Fire and Faith

everything in its path. I tried with everything I had to get up and walk to the front door of the apartment. When I finally made it the front door, I was very weak. I was not even sure if I was going to be able to make it down the stairs from the second floor. As I made my way down the stairs I could not even remember where I parked my car. I must have walked around for what seemed like hours to me, trying to find my car. When I did find it, it was nowhere even close to where I thought it was parked. When I got into the car, there was barely enough gas in the car to make it home. I'd had a full tank when I got there seventeen days ago. I do not know if I drove it or if someone else was driving it. All I knew was that all the gas was gone.

Chapter 23

During the thirty-minute drive home I had a lot on my mind. My major

concern was trying to stay awake long enough to make it back to my

wife's sister's house. The other concern was that I hoped they'd let me

back in. The last time I was there had not been so pretty with the huge

fight, all the names I called Debbie's sister, and the fight with her

husband. Also I had to face my children. To be truthful I did not

deserve any of the above mentioned. I had hit the bottom and now I

had to crawl back home and accept what was coming. For me, the

most important thing on my mind was to make sure that my daughter

Breanne was okay. Then I would deal with the rest of my mess.

I was so scared to show myself, and I knew I looked like a mess. I

had not bathed and I smelled horrible because I was on the floor for so

long and was sweating during my time there. In fact, if Breanne was

not hurt, I probably would not even have come home. I want everyone

who is reading this to understand that it's not that I didn't love my

children or wife. It's just that being an addicted to the drug takes over

everything. Then every once in a while I would come to the realization

of what I was doing and I would feel horrible. I would be so disgusted

with myself for hurting my family and myself. I would look at my

Fire and Faith

children and see how I was hurting and robbing them of my love, and again I would begin to feel guilty for it. Then I would get right back on that cycle and get high again to numb myself of my convictions.

I remember I pulled up in front of my wife sister's house where my wife and children were living. It was about three-0'clock in the afternoon on a warm day. The front windows of the house were open and I could hear my kids in the house talking. I must have sat in the car for about ten minutes debating whether or not I should go to the door. I lacked the courage because of my guilt and shame. I felt like a complete disgrace! During that ten-minute sit in the car, many thoughts ran through my mind. I kept coming to the thought that I did not deserve the love of my wife and children. I felt as if I'd gone too far with my bad behavior. I also believed that my oldest daughter would never forgive me. She was seven years old, and I know for myself, I had very clear memories of when I was seven. Naturally, I thought she would hold a lot against me. I also believed that I blew any kind of trust with both of my daughters as well as my wife. To be truthful, I honestly thought of just starting the car and driving away. I genuinely felt as if there was no way of saving anything. I was broken at that point. I was at that bottom of bottoms!

Fire and Faith

I leaned forward and turned the key to the off position and slid the key out of the ignition. I seemed to have enough courage to get out of the car, and make my way up the driveway. As I got closer to the front door I could hear a blow-dryer running and I assumed it was my wife in the bathroom doing her hair. The weird part to this is that I could hear a life going on inside that I was not part of. It was a life that I wanted so badly to be a part of. But instead, I could not help but have a life of banishment from my family. As I got closer to the door my heart started to race and my hands started to sweat. The screen door was shut but the front door was open and I could smell a home cooked meal being prepared. I could hear my children talking in the other room, and I could hear the radio on in the kitchen. I reached out and knocked at the door.

I waited as I saw my brother-in-law rounding the corner of the kitchen. I was so scared at that moment, and I was not sure what was going to happen. He had every right to shut the door in my face, considering what I did that night when I left. I was so horrible to him and his wife the night of the fight. I was also so horrible for leaving and not returning home. Let's be serious about this, I had been gone for seventeen days with no communication to anyone in my family. My brother-in-law opened the screen door and looked at me. It seemed like forever to me that he stared at me, but it was only seconds. I said to him "Is my wife here?" At that moment he opened his arms and hugged me and said "Your home." He told me that my wife was in the bedroom with my daughters.

I made my way down the hallway and rounded the corner to my wife standing in the bathroom doing her hair. She looked into the mirror to see me standing there and her face went to tears. My two daughters came out of the bedroom across the hall and yelled "Daddy!" When I looked at Breanne I saw what the cat had done to her head and face. She had been holding our cat and something scared him and he had clawed his way up Breanne's face and head cutting her eye and scalp severely. Fortunately his claw did not destroy her eye. After looking at Breanne, and my other beautiful daughter Morgan, I could feel the tears start to leak from my eyes. I really did not know what to do. I was expecting to be yelled at, or told to leave, but they loved me instead.

We walked into the bedroom and sat down on the bed. My wife had questions for me, but I was so weak from everything that had happened to me and the stress of coming home, I just wanted to sleep. I hugged and kissed my kids and my wife as well and they let me sleep for a couple of hours until dinner was ready. The wonderful part to this was

Fire and Faith

that everyone had questions for me, but no one asked them until I was properly rested. My brother-in-law told me that he would be waking me up in the morning to start the day right, as I excused myself from the table after dinner. My wife and I and the girls went to our bedroom just after dinner. I wanted to look at what happened to Breanne. When I finally got a good look at her, I could see the damage that had happened. My little girl was so tough and she told me that she was OK, but I knew that she was in pain.

We stayed in the bedroom that night and we watched television. I do not think I was awake for long before I finally fell asleep. It only seemed like a moment had passed and my brother-in-law Owen was waking me up. He told me to "Get up and come and eat some breakfast." Owen was determined to help me through the sobering process. He had my days planned to help me get sober. He made sure I ate three meals a day, and planned small jobs around the house to keep me busy. He also took me to the doctors for a check-up to make sure I was ok. The doctor told Owen and I that I was severely underweight and that I needed rest, food and most of all stay sober.

For the next several months I continued to stay sober and even started going to church where I dedicated my life to Christ. My wife's sister Barbara was so proud of me and I actually started to feel as if I

295

Fire and Faith

had a purpose. Owen even took me to a Christian retreat the last a 3 days. I was actually put to work there in helping out. I was doing all the registration and checking the men in. During this time I ran into a gentleman that worked there and he was a permanent live-in. He had a problem with meth as well and his was so bad that he could not live in any other place than that. He told me the best solution for not to get high was to take him out of the element. To this day I often think of him, and pray that he been empowered to move on. As far as the rest of the retreat, I ended up really sick and I stayed in bed for the next three days. I can honestly say that it was okay though. I could still hear the worship team playing their music, and that was wonderful. When we came back I was sold on church.

In this process I talked with my wife about a lot of the things that I did and what happened to me. I told her some of things that happened and other things I did not talk about. The funny part was that sometimes I would start to tell her things, and she would stop me and say "You do not have to tell me anything because I have imagined the worst and have forgiven you for them." What an amazing display of forgiveness.

During this time I took a job a local supermarket and did very well there. I used to work nights there stocking groceries, and to be honest I

Fire and Faith

really loved it there. I used to walk home in the mornings from work. On the way home I spotted a boxing gym and thought to myself, I should join this gym and learn to fight the correct way. I started immediately. I walked into this gym thinking I was going to kick everyone's butt. Boy was I wrong! I had so much to learn and this was nothing like street fighting. I could not even jump rope. I stayed at this gym for a while and my life with my wife was going great.

In fact we were doing so well between my wife and I working, we decided to get our own place and try and have another baby. We accomplished the baby part, but finding a place was a lot more difficult. We were living in California and were close to the beach. Everything in that area was much more expensive than Arizona had been. We also had another situation. We were told that my grandfather's health was failing. This was all according to my grandmother at the time. So after careful consideration we knew that we would never be able to afford a home in California, and I also wanted to be close to my grandfather, so we decided to move back to Arizona. I know my wife did not want to come back to Arizona, but she followed me anyway.

Chapter 24

I honestly thought I was strong enough to return, but the truth was I was not. After moving back to Arizona I got caught up with old friends and old habits. It was not long before I was disappearing at night and leaving to get high. We did however start attending a local church and although I would attend the service high, we still went. I was leading a double life again. I was pretending not to be high and trying to keep a job. On the outside, I looked OK for a while. Eventually I started losing weight and the dark circles under my eyes and sunken face started to show. People began to talk at church. As months passed, I met some really good people at church that had a lot of patience with me and who actually saw the good in me.

One of the men that I met at church was Donald. He and his father owned a construction company called Level Up. Donald hired me to basically be a jack of all trades. It was a good job and I learned more than anything else. Donald and his dad were decent to me, and to this day I have a wonderful relationship with them. However, while I was working for them I was making money, and it was very easy for me to lie to my wife about the hours I worked. So I was able to skim my checks and buy dope. What I did not know was there was another gentleman on the crew that used to do the same dope I did and he could recognize in me.

It was not long though and I started to make excuses as to why I could not make it to work. Do not get me wrong, I loved this job because of the very people that surrounded me there, but once more the dope superseded everything. During the day I would look for reasons to leave work early and some occasion I would get dope on Friday and not come until Monday night. The problem was the guy I mentioned before. His name was Curtis and he could spot if I was high in a second. So sometimes I would call from a payphone to Donald and tell him that I was sick. One day Donald and I were driving from one job to the other and he told me that he knew 10 people that did meth and only one made it off the drug for good. (Now he knows two.) I believe though, it was those types of people that I met at church that had their hand in my healing.

One of these people at church led a men's group called "Men of Valor" or MOV. This was the beginning of really understanding what it would take to be a better man. But, I was not ready to be that man. (I will discuss Men of Valor later.) I was not ready to forgive myself and everyone from my past. And that was my down fall. I continued on the path of self-destruction for about another six months. I

Fire and Faith

remember one night I had been gone for several days, and I wanted to come home. It was about two-o'clock in the morning and I was on my way home, but I did not have the courage to actually pull in the driveway and go in the house.

I was embarrassed and filled with shame for going out and getting high. As I drove past my house like all the other times, there was a big piece of paper taped to the garage door. The note said "It's ok, just come in. I forgive you." That note seemed to be there every time I would leave for a couple of days to go and get high. But on this particular night I did not pull into the driveway, instead I drove to the corner market. I sat in the parking lot in the car for quite some time. I felt myself going down the same path of destruction as I did so many times in the past. I decided that the only way to get out of this was to turn myself into some type of clinic or rehab center to get help.

I started with the phone book that was attached to the payphone and looked up different places to go for help. Every place I called was either out of state and wanted money or insurance to pay for my help. The others simply wanted cash before I could be accepted into a program. I understand that they needed money, but I also believe that someone wanting help is far more important than 6000 dollars up front. So the next thing that came to mind was to turn myself into the local

Fire and Faith

police department. I called them to tell them where I was at and that I

had a large amount of meth on me still and that I wanted to be arrested.

I told the officer that I had a loaded 9mm in my car, a large amount of

dope, a pipe and I had been high for days, and on top of all that, I did

not trust myself to not hurt someone.

When I spoke to the police dispatcher, he told me to call back in an

hour because they were in the middle of a shift change. He gave me

the name of the officer to contact and that he would be the one to talk

to. I could not believe what I was hearing. I was turning myself in

with one of the most deadly drugs in my possession, yet they told me to

call back later. He actually thought I would the 45 minutes and call

back, or he thought I was bluffing. The truth is I was so blown away

by that response it actually took my mind off hurting someone or doing

more drugs. I sat there in the car completely out of options. Then it

occurred to me, I live right by a fire station, so I immediately drove

there and knocked at the door.

I will never forget that moment. I'd been trying to hide what I had

been doing for so long, and now I was about to tell a complete stranger

that I needed help. It was so early the sun was even completely up yet

and it was still pretty dark out. The door opened and there was a

woman standing there asking how she could help me. She was a

Fire and Faith

paramedic and she was willing to help. I told her that I was high on meth and that I needed help. She immediately brought me into the building without question and got her co-workers to come and check me out. They took me into the backroom and started taking my vitals. They were astonished to find my heart rate pumping at a speed that would kill any other man, yet I was very calm.

This was a blessing for me and for the fire department. They were asking me questions about meth. They explained to me that most calls they get about someone on meth is usually someone who is out of control and cannot answer any questions. They were amazed that I was even alive with the amount of meth that I had done. (As a side note, this is not a bragging moment for me, but more of an informative moment so you understand how much I had done.) There seemed to be no limit with me. My wife once told me that, "I was an all or nothing kind of guy." I guess she was right; it was just unfortunate that I could not be "all in" with something good. After about forty-five minutes of questioning and checking my vitals to make sure I would be alright, they called my wife to come and get me. I left there that morning with a feeling that I was not familiar with.

I was starting to feel like there was going to be a serious change in my life but I could not put my finger on it yet. We had been back for

Fire and Faith

over a year in Arizona and I was right back where I started again with the drugs. This time however I was getting deeper and deeper into the drug world. I was moving my way up and actually cooking meth. This seemed to be the path of no return. Everyone I knew and met in this realm was either going to prison or would die. There was no in-between. My entire world was falling apart, and there was no way that I would be able to lie my way out of this. I was getting in deep with people that were absolutely no good for me or anyone else for that matter. Everything seemed out of control and I did not know how to get out. I guess you could say that they were the heavy hitters of the drug world. (You could use your imagination about the people I was involved with and you probably are right.) (So, no more is to be said about those people.)

I straightened up for a short period of time though. I started getting cleaned up, and I decided to get job. I worked a local grocery store at night as a stocking clerk. I did this for a couple of months and before I knew it, I was made assistant manager, and four months after that I was promoted to grocery manager. This lasted for a while and I was doing really, really well. As long as I stayed out of the areas that were trouble for me, I was fine. The problem with that was the store transferred me to a new store that was in a bad part of town. I was not strong enough

Fire and Faith

to stay sober. It was not long before I was able to get dope once again. I found myself right where I left off. I found myself in the bathroom at work getting high. I was starting to slip-up at work. Showing up late, or not showing up at all became the norm. Eventually I just stopped going. Then I started not coming home for days on end.

My wife started to reach out to the men that were in my men's group. Well actually, she reached out to the instructor of the course. He called me and told me to call him before I left to get high. (Like that was going to happen.) I think he actually believed that he could talk me out of getting high! I left home one night after scoring some really killer dope and a lot of it. There was actually enough for me to be high three days. I had a quarter ounce of the best glass in Arizona. After the third day of out and about, I found my attitude to be very explosive. I thought to myself, I literally could commit murder. I was just waiting for the right person to cut me off on the road, or flip me off, and that would have been it. I decided to call the instructor of the class to tell him the frame of mind that I was in. He told me to come over to his house, and that he would help me. There was another man there, and he was able to reach me. But it came with a cost. Before I knew it my anger and rage was full-vent at that man. Fortunately I did not catch him. But he did help me to see the light.

Fire and Faith

Fortunately for me, I met some heavy hitters in the spiritual world.
To this day, these key people are active in my life and are close friends.
Each one of them, at some point, I believe said something to me that
would soon add up to help me find the answer I was looking for. Other
words it was no single action that came me from men, but the seed that
was sown from all the people helped me along the way. I met one
other man that told me forgiveness was my answer. At the time I was
in a drug and alcohol class that was operating out of another church.
He told me that forgiveness was my answer to freedom. He explained
that I needed to forgive everyone that had wronged me in my life.
When he said that I thought that would not be a problem. Then he said
I needed to be forgiven by all the people that I have wronged. When he
said that, I laughed and said to him "Good luck with that!" He even
went on to say that I needed to seek forgiveness from my dad, and
believe it or not, that was one of the core issues my problem. I already
had the Lord in my heart, but now the Lord sent the final piece in the
puzzle.

When I started out on this mission of forgiveness I really thought
this would be no big deal. The problem was I never in my 38 years
ever truly forgiven someone. I did not even know what forgiveness
looked like. After struggling with this for a while, I came to the

Fire and Faith

realization that forgiveness did not mean to forget. Forgiveness is

being able to re-visit the past, but not have the pain. I had to think of

through my own children. This is what God pointed out to me. I

looked at like if one of my daughters said or did something wrong, I

could not hold a grudge. Meaning it was easy to forgive my daughters

for their mistakes, and then I should be able to forgive others.

Although the problems were small it was still about forgiveness. I did

forgive others, but the challenge was forgiving me for the things I did.

For me forgiveness came from grieving. I have to say that this was

a giant in my life that I thought would never rest. I really looked inside

of myself and found that the child in me was suffering from what had

happened and was still hurt. My child was wounded, hungry, hurt, and

cold. My child never grew up because I never grieved from what my

father had been like to me. In fact I never really grieved for anything

that happened in my life. Then the second major hurdle did not surface

until I sat in a men's group with my peers. The facilitator looked at me

one night and basically "read my mail." Meaning he saw the wounded

child in me and knew that I had a deep dark secret.

After several minutes of poking and prodding around in my feelings,

it finally surfaced. My past rapes came out in a violent and angry way.

It was so bad that I did not trust myself, and the facilitator surrounded

Fire and Faith

himself with friends for protection. I will tell you now, there were

moments when I wanted to get up and leave. There were also moments

that I wanted to get up and beat the men that were there in the room

with me that night half to death. It was bad enough that this happened

to me; there was no way that I wanted the rest of the world to know it

happened to me. I spent most of my life being tough and rough and

now I felt as if I was not. I was vulnerable and that was the best

medicine for me. I felt like I had been ganged-up on. I felt helpless. I

felt weak. I felt angry. Most of all, I felt scared.

I had always felt that being raped had been my fault. I always felt

that I should have been strong enough to get away. I always felt that

because I did not do anything to get away made me less of a human

being. Because of those feelings I could never come into manhood.

There was a child that lived in me who was frightened; a child that

could never grow up and be a man. The facilitators name was Paul and

he asked me if the situation happened to one of my daughters, would I

blame her. Meaning if a man raped my daughter would I believe it was

her fault. The answer was an immediate "No!" I told him that I would

feel horrible for not protecting them enough and I would probably kill

the man that hurt them. The truth is I learned a lot that night that set me free. I also learned to forgive the men in my life that had raped me. It took time, but I did it.

All my life I grew up thinking, and believing I had nothing to offer the world. I had to basically pretend my way through life, because I felt that I had no value to anyone or anything. I also grew up believing that I could not let things go for too long, because I always felt things eventually would turn bad. If relationships, jobs, living, or anything was going well for too long, I would eventually try to ruin it by through my behavior, or simply abandon them or it. When it came to girls, I had a harder time "abandoning" them anyway. No matter what age I was, I did not handle hurting someone feelings very well. I am not saying I did not hurt anyone's feelings. What I am saying is that it really hurt my heart too. I now have mended the relationships that I could. I now have a relationship with Bob as well and it is a decent one as well. The only relationship that has not been restored is the one with my dad, and not at my fault. I have tried, but he refuses to talk to me. I know that God has changed all of this for me and I believe that He will change the things that I can't.

What is really amazing is that through the garbage and trouble that I was put myself and everyone else through, I met some wonderful and influential people that did not give up on me. I have to say no one

Fire and Faith

single person had the magic words to me that made me sober up and change my life around. I honestly believe it was a multitude of wonderful people, with wonderful insight and key words followed by love. I also firmly believe that God was the ultimate changing factor. I believe that God set these wonderful people out in the world, and He carefully placed them in my life.

There was something else that God did in my life other than healing me from addiction and pain. I was not going to put this in the book only because I felt that it was too personal. But I have to say that God did something else that I believe changed everything in my life. Not only did He give me my family back, but He now lives in my family. He met me in a way that I cannot describe. He met me like the sun meets the day. He was gentle, caring, loving and most all a father to me. I can't explain it, but I know He has met me on every level. I have always had "daddy issues". Without words, but whispers, he has confirmed His love as a father would to me. What a beautiful thought it is. It is much more than a feeling. I know my Father in Heavens love just as you know that you are reading this book.

Additionally, I believe that there is no such thing as an addict. I believe we all have addictive tendencies, but that is as far as it goes. The truth is no one deserves to be called an addict. If we are to be

Fire and Faith

labeled, our true label is that we are children of God. By labeling

someone an addict is only adding a challenge for someone to

overcome, and with that word "challenge" leads to the possibility of

failure. In fact, in the Christian world the term "challenge" is used

quite frequently and that is wrong. Christians like to say, "I challenge

you to read this passage in the bible, or I challenge you to change a

certain behaviors. As I mentioned before, a challenge leaves the

possibility of failure. Instead I like to use the word "encouragement".

Encouragement is like the coach we all need in life. Jesus himself used

words of encouragement. I truly believe in my heart of hearts there are

no "bad" people. I believe there are only people making bad decisions

I want to explain to everyone that is reading this book, that since I

was delivered from my abusive drug use, I have, with the help from

God, put my life back together. I made the decision to enroll at Liberty

University and obtain my Bachelor's degree in psychology and

Christian counseling. I am now a senior, and I will graduate with my

bachelor's degree in Psychology with a specialization in Christian

counseling. I even made the Dean's list with a 3.75 GPA. (Since I

never finished high school, I am very proud of this accomplishment.) I

am also currently enrolled at Liberty University in the Master's degree

program, and will matriculate next year. I would also like to mention,

Fire and Faith

that anyone can accomplish this and more. I was never a good student. In fact I was considered at one point not a good person. The truth is that everyone is good. There are no bad people in this world; there are just good people that are lost and doing bad things. A friend of mine Paul Crouch (and not the one on television) said, "Most people believe that they are the mistake, and not 'I made a mistake'." Big difference!

Most important though, is to seek out the heart of God and gain understanding of His position on forgiveness. For me, forgiveness does not mean forgetting, whether in the secular world, or the Christian world. We should never forget, because remembering is the vital tool for learning purposes. In the bible we are to be aware of deceivers, and we forget every time we forgive, we learn nothing. God wants us to forgive, and be able to reflect on the past, but not experience the pain. That is forgiveness!

Fire and Faith

Family Picture by Audra Kimball

Poem by Daughter Morgan Kimball

Here I am writing this poem

Happiness seems to bloom in this home

When I was a kid my dad would brush my hair

And when it hurt he would spank the brush against the rocking chair

Dad, you've been here all along

Thank you for making our family so strong

Joy is what this family brings

You've taught me many things.

I love you dad.

Fire and Faith

Thoughts to my daughter Breanne

My dearest Breanne, you are the beat of my heart and my miracle here on earth. My love for you is boundless and it is forever echoing in the universe and in the heavens above. I thank you for the privilege to have another chance to be a father to you. I have made mistakes all through my life, and I will most definitely make more mistakes as my life goes on. I am far from being perfect and I accept that. I spent years of your life being high, and although I was there physically, I was not there in full for you with my heart. Do not get me wrong. I have always loved you. In fact one of the main reasons for me to get clean and off drugs was because of you. Through our lives together I made promises, and I have broken those same promises, and for that I am truly sorry. I want you to know that I made a silent promise to you and that was that I would always be there in your time of need. I promised that I would be there to protect you, comfort you, and most importantly share the Lord above with you. I promised that I would do everything in my power to be the best dad that I could for you. In that silent promise was to provide you with all of your needs and desires. I promised to be there when you laugh, cry, smile, and to be there when you accomplish your dreams and goals. Most of all I promise to always speak truth to you.

Fire and Faith

You my dearest Breanne have grown into a wonderful person. You are a wonderful daughter to me. I enjoy watching scary movies with you, or listening to you talk about your day. I love walking down the hallway past your room and I hear your music full blast. I love talking to you about the serious things in life and the not so serious too. What I am really saying to you is that I want to thank you for being you. You are beautiful and never think otherwise. I want to thank you for loving me through the bad and the good of my life. There are not words to describe how much I love you for that. I pray and thank God daily for you. I am truly blessed to call you my daughter. I want you to remember that I do not blame my past for what I did wrong as an adult. I made those bad choices and I am responsible for myself. I told you the same thing long ago; you are responsible for what you do in life and I know that you will do the best you can and do very well. You are beautiful, strong, loving, intelligent, and you know the Father in Heaven. Never forget that. One more thing Breanne, don't ever be afraid to show your love. You have so much love and that is a gift.

Love always forever, your Dad "Hit Me Again Tube Sock"

Fire and Faith

Thoughts to my daughter Morgan

My dearest Morgan, I love you more than words can describe, and I also would like to thank you for the privilege of raising you. In the beginning of your wonderful life I was there, and it was not until sometime later that I started doing the bad things I did. Nevertheless, I wish I had not done those things that I did. I am sorry that I ever hurt you in the way of not being there for you. I know I was there for every school function, and I was physically there for you, but mentally I was not. While I was on drugs Morgan, I was not me. I was there deep down, and I always loved you, but I was not strong enough to beat my addiction with drugs by myself, and I realize that must have been confusing to you. I am sure you thought at some point if I really loved you I would have quit doing drugs and be there as a father, but it was not that simple. What I can say though is that your love, the love of your sisters, and the love from your mother was what helped me through my difficult times.

You and I now have a wonderful relationship and I thank God daily for that. I am also so glad that we have time to be a father and daughter to each other. I am glad that I will be able to be there for you as you grow up in life. You have made me a very proud father, and I thank you for that. Just know Morgan you have so much to offer, and you absolutely

Fire and Faith

deserve the best in life. You are beautiful and I know you can be very kind to others, so don't be afraid to show it. I will tell you the same thing as I told your sisters. You are beautiful, strong; loving, intelligent, forgiving, and you know the Father in Heaven. You have an amazing heart towards other people and do not ever let that harden. You, my dear, are deserving of a wonderful life. Keep your head held high all through life, and smile your way through the tough times. These are the real qualities in life that we all truly need, and everything else is second. I love you so much!

Love always your Dad. "Daddy's Sleepy"

Fire and Faith

Thoughts to my daughter Audra

My dearest daughter Audra I love you so much. You have been a little different with me than your sisters. Mainly because I have been sober for the most part with you. In the very beginning I was still struggling with my addiction, but you were so young, you really don't remember any of it. That is blessing for me. I know that I am hard on you at times, and to be truthful I sometimes realize it. I know that your potential is amazing, and I sometimes think that if I am hard on you that you will go beyond what anyone could have thought of. I think the other reason is because I want you to stay on the straight and narrow just like your sisters need to stay on the straight and narrow. I have the same expectation for you as I do for your sisters, and that is to accomplish as much as you can in life, and really make a difference. It is my pleasure and honor to be a father to such a wonderful daughter.

I know at times I was busy writing this book, as well as, doing my school work. But the time you and I have together is wonderful. We have so much to look forward to still. We have father daughter dances still to come and boyfriends for me to scare and that goes to your sisters as well. The truth is Audra, is that I love that you have to have a daily hug and kiss from me and that you love to tell me stories. I love

Fire and Faith

hanging out watching movies with you. We have something really special and I thank you for that. I have to tell you the same thing I have told your sisters and that is, you are beautiful, strong, loving, intelligent, forgiving, and you know the Father in Heaven. You will find this sentence in your sister's letters as well, but it is true for all of you. I thank God that I have you in my life Audra. I love you so much!

Love always your Dad. "I'm not pretty. Now Stay Down."

Fire and Faith

To my wife

We have been through so much in our lives. I believe that we have probably lived three lifetimes together. I want to thank you for not giving up on me. You have never turned your back on me. You once said to me, that you did not need to hear all the details about the times of addiction, and that you imagined the worst and forgave me for it. What a true testimony of not only faith in Christ, but a beautiful display of forgiveness. You never kicked me out, when I know I for fact I deserved to be kicked out. You have loved me at my worst and at my best. I would say that you have the type of love that Christ would want us to have for one another. What a blessing! I know I am not a very mushy person when it comes to you and me, but I am trying to get better with my transparency. I thank you for your hard work in this relationship as well as the hard work you put in while I went to school and wrote this book. We got something good and we are blessed!

Forever yours,

Joey . . .